Parabl

Northern Seed

Anthology from BBC's *Thought for the Day*

Alastair McIntosh

wild goose

publications

www.**ionabooks**.com

© 2014 Alastair McIntosh

First published 2014 by
Wild Goose Publications, Fourth Floor, Savoy House,
140 Sauchiehall Street, Glasgow G2 3DH, UK,
the publishing division of the Iona Community.
Scottish Charity No. SC003794. Limited Company Reg. No. SC096243.

ISBN 978-1-84952-302-8

Cover image: *The Sower*, by Vincent Van Gogh, June 1888,
supplied by Awesome Art

The publishers gratefully acknowledge the support of the Drummond
Trust, 3 Pitt Terrace, Stirling FK8 2EY in producing this book.

Overseas distribution
Australia: Willow Connection Pty Ltd, Unit 4A, 3–9 Kenneth Road,
Manly Vale, NSW 2093
New Zealand: Pleroma, Higginson Street, Otane 4170, Central Hawkes Bay
Canada: Bayard Distribution, 10 Lower Spadina Ave., Suite 400,
Toronto, Ontario M5V 2Z

Printed by Bell & Bain, Thornliebank, Glasgow

MIX
Paper from
responsible sources
FSC
www.fsc.org   FSC® C007785

For my mother, Jean,
who encouraged me to write when young

Contents

Introduction

'The seed must move from north to south.' These were the words that dropped from the mouth of an old crofter who I found harvesting his fields at Durness one late September's afternoon in 2007.

We were halfway between London and the Arctic Circle. I'd been invited by my friend Mike Merritt to speak at his award-winning John Lennon Northern Lights Festival. Lennon had holidayed in the village as a child. Yoko Ono had endorsed the gig. John's sister Julia Baird was guest of honour. Nizlopi and the Quarrymen (forerunners of the Beatles) were headline acts. And here was this denim-dungareed crofter telling me that he liked to get the seedstock for his oats from Orkney, even further to the north, because this gave his crop the hardiness required to flourish on his weather-blasted ground.

Those words played poetry in my mind. They spoke in metaphor, suggestive of renewal flowing from the wave-washed rural edges to the parched metropolis, and I pondered on another phrase I'd once heard someone use: *'When the centre collapses the periphery becomes central.'*

So it was that the seed of yet another *Thought for the Day* was sown, and as a Free Church clergyman on the Isle of Lewis is fond of saying: *'The field looks no different at the end of a day's sowing, but harvest is the proof of faith.'* As for my linking this to parables, that's because I cut my teeth with liberation theology when I was in my twenties and thirties working in the South Pacific. One day in the Solomon Islands I asked a visionary Catholic priest, Fr John Roughan: *'Why did Jesus talk so much in parables?'*

'A parable,' he mused, 'is an armour-piercing missile. It penetrates the outer crusts of ego and explodes its meaning softly down through ever-deepening layers within the human heart.'

I present *Thought for the Day* on Radio Scotland about ten times a year and, less frequently, *Prayer for the Day* on Radio 4. 'Why privilege religion in public broadcasting?' some ask. Well, why business reports? Why sport? Why not the 'God slot' as a faith reflection on current affairs for listeners to whom it speaks?

As a Quaker, my 'thoughts' are usually Christian but I also love to draw on other faiths based on love. After all, Jesus in John's Gospel said: *'I have other sheep that are not of this fold'* and *'in my father's house are many mansions'*. For me, there's also many windows in those mansions and each lets in the light from its own distinctive angle. None of them is perfect. Some were once meticulously crafted but now the frames have rotted and they rattle in the wind. Others were once blasted through by cannon-ball and yet, given ample time to compost in God's garden, even soils of sourest disposition can issue forth sweet blossom.

The day before I'm due to present a thought one of the editors from the BBC's religion team phones up. We turn over whatever's trending in the news. I try to bring an attitude of spiritual discernment. What matters is not to push a line, but to listen for the promptings of the Spirit; for that of life as love made mani-fest. To me, that inspiration stamps the hallmark on a good *Thought for the Day*. We'll settle on a topic and by early afternoon I'll e-mail through to my editor a first draft. It's only a single page and yet, as the layers and resonances build up, it often takes me all day to fine-tune.

Delivery goes out live from Good Morning Scotland's studio. The night before, I set my alarm to rise at some ungodly hour. I know I'll keep on waking up for worry of sleeping in and so my wife, long-suffering, evicts me to the spare room. It's not so much the fear of letting down the nation that bugs me. More, the fear of what my octogenarian mother in Stornoway would say. Just imagine her getting behind the microphone in riposte. That would make a cracking *Thought for the Day*!

Over the past nine years I've produced a hundred broadcasts, and what a privilege it is to work with these women and men at the BBC who have helped so much to polish up my scripting and intonation. Sometimes there's an 'ouch' when they pull me up, but I must admit: they're nearly always spot on.

The anthology in your hands was suggested, selected and lightly edited by Neil Paynter at the Iona Community. I thank him and his sharp eye warmly. But let me close with one last word from Durness.

Some weeks after my northern seed broadcast I was e-mailed by a local lass called Sophie Anne Macleod. She was seeking a quote for her classroom project about the Northern Lights event.

Bursting with youthful enthusiasm she said: 'The old man that you were talking to is my high school bus driver, Michael. I see him every day.'

Now, to me there's something curiously armour-piercing in such a simple human connection. It brings an honest-to-life quality that often grounds *Thought for the Day* in the plainsong truths of real people in real places in real time.

I listen to my many co-presenters, and their best thoughts are far more than mere descriptions or opinion. They're deeper ways of seeing and being. They're observations that have required a spiritual presence to the undercurrents of a situation. That is what cracks the husk around the hardy grain and, once winnowed with the editing team, reveals life's inner kernel.

I watch some of those kernels grind to flour and rise to bread '*in memory of me*'. I watch others bubble in the ferment of the copper pot and trickle through as essence from the winding tube. That's a *Thought for the Day* at its very best. The distillation of the land itself and all that it contains.

A form of working in the Spirit – I'd call it Scotland's other whisky industry.

Said Luke and Matthew: 'For *the Son of Man comes eating and drinking.*'

Eat, drink, and I sincerely hope that you'll find savour in these *Parables of Northern Seed.*

Alastair McIntosh,
Govan, 2014

Calming the tempest

I was on a train in England last week when a complete stranger sat down and immediately started talking about the need for radical government action on climate change.

I was puzzled by his passion, until I asked where he came from.

'Ah ... I'm from Tornado Land,' he replied. 'You see, I'm one of those people who had their roof blown off by the Birmingham tornado!'

Now, it would be bad science to link last month's tornado or this week's American hurricane directly to the effects of global warming. All we can say is that many scientists consider freak weather will get more and more the norm if we continue pumping greenhouse gases into the atmosphere.

We need to tackle the root causes of climate change with greater intelligence, with better public understanding of science and with tough political will. But we also need greater compassion to face the suffering. And of course, there'll be many who ask, 'Why does God allow it?'

It's the same question we heard after the Indian Ocean tsunami. 'Why?'

But if we believe that God unfolds this universe, do we really expect a paternalistic hand to intervene in the weather and geological processes?

Should the voice of the Almighty have boomed down over New Orleans, instructing city planners never to build below sea level?

Or is the real spiritual challenge to develop the courage and intelligence that can face crisis, suffering and death? Is it to open our hearts, expand our minds and deepen our humanity, so that we get wise?

Perhaps it's a living spirituality and not just good buildings insurance that's needed if the roof blows off.

The core of common humanity

Multiculturalism has become such a hot issue because today's world has shrunk so much. People of diverse cultures and religions live side by side. But that doesn't of course mean that they experience equality. For example, across Britain Muslims have an unemployment rate that is three times higher than the national average.

This past week saw the launch in Scotland of a new study, *The Dream Job Report*. It asks this question: Can every Scot, no matter where they originally come from, aspire to their 'dream job' and so fulfil their human potential?

The report is full of eye-openers. Devout young Muslims from Glasgow Mosque say that, yes, they must have time to pray at work, but this is precisely what helps them to be honest, hardworking and loyal employees.

Here in Scotland we've long believed that what matters more than where you come from is 'a man's a man for a' that'. This, surely, is the way forward. It allows us to hold fast to our traditional anchor points but equally to be open to the whole world.

There's a wonderful passage by the late Iain Crichton Smith that reaches to the core of such common humanity. Although he's speaking about folk displaced from the Isle of Lewis to the city, it could equally apply to any one of us, whatever our ethnic origins. Here's what he says:

Sometimes when I walk the streets of Glasgow I see old women passing by, bowed down with shopping bags, and I ask myself: 'What force made this woman what she is? What is her history?' It is the holiness of the person we have lost, the holiness of life itself, the inexplicable mystery and wonder of it, its strangeness, its tenderness.[1]

Note:

1. From Iain Crichton Smith's essay 'Real people in a real place', in his collection *Towards the Human*, Macdonald Publishers, 1986, Lines Review Editions

Profoundly interconnected

I'm not given to having nightmares, but the other day, when my wife and I were staying on Iona, I found myself having one that went on and on …

I was looking east from Glasgow. In the far distance was an industrial complex and houses, including a couple of tower blocks. Suddenly the complex blew up and moments later the tower blocks and everything else cracked and collapsed, like in those horrendous images of the Twin Towers attack.

Something massively terrible had happened and I knew that social mayhem would follow. I tried to find my wife to escape, but she was gone and there was no escape.

As I woke up, the vivid intensity and duration of the dream left me unsettled. I told my wife that I even wondered if something had happened in the world. It was another 24 hours before we heard news of the Pakistan earthquake. The dream had taken place pretty much simultaneously.

Now, there are plenty of times that dreams have only an imagined connection to reality. It's safest to assume they're just coincidences. But at the same time, in many parts of the world a dream like I've just described would seem unexceptional.

It's only our modern minds that see human beings so individualistically. In other world views, humanity is profoundly interconnected. *'Ask not for whom the bell tolls; it tolls for thee.'* We're members one of another, branches on the vine of life, and such is the spiritual basis of community.

As we dig deep into our pockets, this time for Pakistan, it's easy to feel compassion fatigue. But just consider the possibility that all humanity is joined like the fingers of one hand. This is what love implies, and this is what opens the heart to wash compassion fatigue away.

'Hold fast'

Today my thought is from another man, who fought injustice all his life. Yesterday in Lewis, we laid to rest Colin Macleod of Govan's GalGael Trust.[1] Back in July, during the G8 summit in Gleneagles, Colin recorded a Thought for the Day which had to be dropped because of the London bombings. But his words to the powerful are timeless, and we're going to play them now, in his memory:

I'm going to tell you a wee story that I sometimes tell my kids. It comes from the Clan Macleod tradition. Many years ago there was a big feast at a clan gathering in Argyll, a kind of Highland G8. Right in the middle was a wooden stake with a poor clansman tied to it.

Word was, his only crime had been to take a deer from the hill to feed his family. Now, as a punishment, he was to be gored to death by a wild bull for the entertainment of all. But nobody said anything. Naebody, that is, until the chief of the Clan Macleod could stomach his dram no longer.

Quietly he stepped forward and faced the host. 'Why don't you let the man go,' he suggested, 'as a gesture of your generosity?'

The host raised his arm. He pointed to the man at the stake. 'You can secure his freedom, but only if you can stop the bull.'

The gate was thrown open. The bull charged. Quicker than thought, Macleod leapt into its path. He grasped it by the horns. With all his power he wrestled it. At that, the crowd erupted, 'Hold fast! Hold fast!' And he held fast.

The captive was set free and there was great feasting – and what a party they had that night.

And to this day the motto of Clan Macleod is 'Hold Fast'.

This is how it is with the G8 today. The poor are tied to the stake.

Our leaders have a chance to show whether their power is for greed or for service. They must decide whether or not to confront poverty and help end these injustices.

Let the cry of the people be heard: 'Hold fast! Hold fast!'

Note:

1. Colin Macleod founded the GalGael Trust in 1997, along with his wife, Gehan. Growing out of the Pollok Free State motorway protest, GalGael's aim is to tackle poverty and hopelessness, helping people to give expression to their fundamental humanity. It draws inspiration from George MacLeod's maxims 'Glory to God in the High St' and 'Work as worship' (www.galgael.org).

Good luck, bad luck

As the year draws to an end, my thoughts turn to those for whom this has not been a good year. On a world scale, it was as if the whole planet shuddered as the tsunami receded, New Orleans went six feet under, and the poorest of the poor endured the Pakistan earthquake. It all made me think about a fable that speaks of keeping going.

An old man in ancient China had tamed a wild horse. It was his pride and joy, but someone left the gate open and it ran off back to the herd.

Everybody in the village came round saying, 'We are sorry, old man. What bad luck.'

But the old man replied, 'Bad luck, good luck: who is really to know?'

That night the horse returned, bringing with it the entire wild herd. Someone quickly shut the gate, and the village awoke – thrilled to find there'd be horses for all.

'What good luck you've had, old man!' they said. And he said, 'Good luck, bad luck: who is really to know?'

Later on, the old man's son tried breaking in a noble stallion. But it threw him off and broke his leg.

The people said, 'Who will plough your fields now, old man? What bad luck.'

And the old man smiled thinly: 'Bad luck, good luck: who is really to know?'

In the wee small hours that night the village was awakened by the emperor's men. They press-ganged every able-bodied youth to fight a terrible war from which most would never return.

But the son with the broken leg was spared. And so, good luck, bad luck … and when life hits any one of us with its ups and downs, we can never really be sure of deeper meanings.

All we can do is try to keep an open heart. And when we're totally confused and faced only with darkness, remain open to possibility; and seek an opening of the way.

On the death of Coretta Scott King

The same time this week as news broke of the 100th UK soldier to die in Iraq, the world also learned of the moving on from this life of Mrs Coretta Scott King, widow of the American civil rights leader Dr Martin Luther King.

I once spent several days with a close co-worker of the King family. He was a white American who'd held special responsibility for training people in nonviolent defence for when they were faced with aggressive police and the lynch mobs of the Ku Klux Klan at civil rights marches.

'What exactly was the role of white folks like you in those marches?' I asked him.

'We took on being the human shields,' he told me. 'When we saw a black marcher getting beaten up, we'd run and lay our bodies over theirs. Then others would come and place themselves over us so that the kicking got shared.'

He said that it undermined the very spirit of violence. It confused the racial stereotypes and turned the bravado of the violent into cause for shame. It made them turn and think again.

When Coretta Scott King was phoned with the news that her husband had been assassinated, she said it was a call she'd subconsciously waited for all their married lives. But did she feel bitter? No. She said, *'Hate is too great a burden to bear. It injures the hater more than the hated.'*

And she set up the King Center for Nonviolent Social Change, aimed at exposing the links between the structural injustice of poverty and violence in streets and homes, breaking the consequent spiral by which violence feeds further violence, like petrol on a fire, and healing the wound by substituting the love of power with the power of love.

She said, *'The greatness of a community is most accurately measured by the compassionate actions of its members.'* That's the message left by this great black woman today.

Of chaps and maps

When I was at school in the '60s, history was about chaps and geography about maps. We had one particularly dour history teacher with a fetish for ancient battles of a ferocity equalled only by his own sadism. When we failed to memorise dates by rote he'd pull out the belt like a gun from its holster and thwack our trembling hands. Little wonder I migrated from chaps to maps at the earliest opportunity!

But it's very different today, and yet history's being dropped from some school timetables. This week members of the Scottish Association of Teachers of History met MSPs to explain their concern. Modern history teaches children how to evaluate evidence. Pupils are taught to ask questions about what counts as a valid source of information. Who was behind it? Were they reporting or interpreting? And what axes were being ground?

Such questions show children how to think clearly. They're skills that transfer far beyond the history class and are of equal importance to the lawyer evaluating witnesses as to the ordinary citizen trying to understand what's behind conflicting ideas and traditions in the world around them.

Even deeper than that, historical insight shapes our sense of identity. It reveals stories that speak of our past and these shape vision that guides our future. When I talk to young men I find that many are desperate for an identity that can give them values and pride with which to navigate that future. Just yesterday I spoke to one in Govan who said he used to be up to the eyes in sectarianism. 'What changed you?' I asked; and he said, 'I simply learned there was a bigger world than a bigoted one.'

History well taught can give an identity that's strong precisely because it's self-critical and has empathy for others. That's why Scotland's youth needs history, and if its axed, the nation will suffer.

Seeds of peace

Growing up on the Isle of Lewis I used to work summers as a ghillie on the salmon lochs. These were fished by masters of the universe – aristocrats, magnates and military men – and as I'd row the boat about, there was nothing my youthful mind liked better than to cast out a line to the retired generals and try to catch a real-life war story.

I remember asking one general what was the greatest bravery he'd ever seen. 'This will surprise you, Alastair,' he said, 'but it was the Friends Ambulance Unit. They were Quaker pacifists who showed incredible courage in rescuing the wounded of both sides from the front line.'

Yesterday saw the release from captivity of Norman Kember, a member of a Christian Peacemaker Team which had included American Quaker Tom Fox, who was murdered.

Like the Friends Ambulance Unit, these men had chosen to stand in the way of unthinkable violence. Their witness also included advocacy for families whose loved ones had disappeared into the chaotic jails of occupied Iraq.

Professor Kember and his team understood the risks. Like soldiers, they were willing to die for their beliefs, but the difference was that they refused to kill for them.

Jesus was their inspiration. When the soldiers of the Roman occupation arrived for the final showdown, Jesus said, *'Put away your sword, Peter … we will have no more of this.'*

Many will question whether Professor Kember was not just a well-meaning fool. They'll ask if his ordeal achieved anything.

Well, recent months have seen Christians, Jews and Muslims alike praying and campaigning for his release. They've included

the Muslim Association of Britain, the Egyptian Muslim Brother-
hood, and those Britons released from Guantánamo Bay.

Is that not something beautiful in the sight of Allah, of God?
Does that not point towards the path of reconciliation? Perhaps
in these ways the seeds of peace are sown.

Conflict is normal

With power struggles rocking the world of politics one thing we
can be sure of is that *conflict* will dominate this week's headlines.

And that's not just in the big scheme of things. Few of us will
escape conflict in our own homes, schools and offices. Indeed,
the big political fights are probably rooted in the fact that any
fool can live in conflict, but it takes guts to live in peace.

I take a special interest in Scottish communities undergoing land
reform; in their aspirations for security of tenure, for cultural
cohesion and local economic development. Type 'land reform'
into the Internet and we're the first country to come up, even
ahead of Zimbabwe! That's because a quarter of a million acres
of Scotland have now been taken into community ownership,
and it's happened bloodlessly.

But there's a downside to such freedom. Some communities
rightly worry that land reform may lift the lid on simmering local
troubles. That's why conflict resolution skills need to be put at
the heart of community empowerment.

The first and most liberating fact about community conflict is
that it's *normal* – provided it's not just for the sake of stirring
things up, it's a healthy sign of folk finding their voices.

Conflict becomes most toxic when it has stagnated – going

unrecognised or left unprocessed. That's when it turns to corrosive hostility – more the withering hand of passive aggression than the open fist.

And this is why everyone who cares about other people must acquire the courage to sit fearlessly in the fire of conflict. We must insist on exposure to truth and to a no-nonsense empathy that's gives real meaning to trying to love one's neighbour.

In these ways conflict's stinking mess can compost into rich soil from which new life can grow. And remember, it all starts with the disarmingly simple but radically powerful realisation: that *conflict is normal*.

Mistaken identity

A strange thing happened last week. I became temporarily mistaken for a football fan! It was in the columns of that wonderful community newspaper *The Stornoway Gazette*, and somebody had written in having a go at me for supposedly attacking Jack McConnell's lack of support for the English football team.

As it happens, the letter writer had muddled me up with somebody else and they've now graciously apologised. But for a few days, I felt myself uncomfortably thrust into a debate that normally holds no interest for me. You see, I was useless at football in school and spectator sports are just not my religion. Even though I live close enough to Ibrox to hear the cheers go up, I rarely have a clue who's playing.

But the experience of being publicly mistaken for an English supporter last week set me thinking about the passion that the game generates. For those of us who lack the fans' gene, it's easy just to dismiss it all as crowd madness or sublimated aggression. But ask football supporters what really matters to *them*, and some very positive human values emerge: ones that speak powerfully to the need we all have for a sense of identity, a place of belonging, a focus for loyalty and, in a nutshell, community.

Most of us today live in a world where our anchors of community have dragged. We have fewer and fewer shared experiences out of which to forge a group identity. But *football* seems to offer this, and perhaps that's something it can teach those of us who aren't its natural fans.

Maybe in *all* walks of life the name of the big game is to learn how to stand our ground and support our own side, yes, but also to keep the heart open with some empathy for the other side too. After all, they're only expressing the same needs and values as we have.

For humanity to shine through we have to become big enough to *respect* our opponents. That's the measure of our greatness; the measure of a nation too.

Civilisation begins within

In yesterday's Thought for the Day, Bob Kernohan, the retired editor of the Church of Scotland's magazine, *Life and Work*, asked what we individuals can do about the crisis in the Middle East, and he ended with the quotation: *'Ask not to see the distant scene; one step enough for me.'*

There's something about conflict in the Middle East that touches us very deeply. We know it can hit us in the pocket as petrol prices rise. But there's more. As the poet John Donne put it: *'Never send to know for whom the bell tolls; it tolls for thee.'*

The Middle East has been called 'the cradle of civilisation', and for many people in the West it symbolises the cultural heart of the world. It is the mythical home of Eden, yes, but also of Armageddon. Conflict there spills out from such countries as Lebanon, Israel and Iraq and into our own hearts.

That's why, as Bob Kernohan suggested, it matters to take steps within our own lives. For me, violence in the world is like a jigsaw. Consciously or unconsciously we all carry the pieces. If you and I can start dealing with our complicity, then we help to improve the whole picture.

Recently I witnessed a conflict between two recovering heroin addicts in a hard-pressed quarter of one of our Scottish cities. They'd been set against one another by malicious circumstances and one understandably became so inflamed by the spirit of violence that he procured the means to do something terrible to the other.

But then a wonderful thing happened. Little by little, he softened his anger with a counterbalancing spirit of restraint. At first he was only able to postpone doing his damnedest on an hour-by-hour basis. But gradually, these little steps grew longer, and now both men have made it up with neither going to jail nor hospital.

If ordinary people can find the strength to resolve potentially murderous violence, is there not hope for us all? The cradle of civilisation in the Middle East may be engulfed in strife, but that doesn't mean we should lose faith in humanity.

The misheard bigamist

I read yesterday that the British Army have advised soldiers to limit their bagpipe-playing to under half an hour, because it's as bad as the noise of a chainsaw for people's hearing.

My own ears always prick up at such reports because I've had impaired hearing for the past 5 years. It's probably genetic (though I'd rather add it up to a misspent youth on Stornoway's disco scene). Hearing loss is affecting people in growing numbers. According to the General Household Survey, 20% of men and 15% of women report difficulties in later middle age.

In Scotland we're blessed with state-of-the-art NHS audiologists. My consultant is in a wheelchair, and I asked him which he'd prefer: to have a hearing or a mobility issue. He said 'mobility', because, as Helen Keller, who became both blind and deaf, put it, *'Blindness cuts you off from things; [but] deafness cuts you off from people.'*

That's the galling bit. For me, diminished hearing is a social disability. Mind you, it can have an amusing side. I remember once lecturing to a church group and being asked a question by a man who introduced himself as a 'bigamist'. I answered as delicately as I could, only to have him loudly declare: 'I said I'm a *botanist!*'

You can never fully correct permanent hearing loss, but modern digital hearing aids do a pretty amazing job. When I first got mine, my biggest obstacle was embarrassment. Would people stare? Would my wife still fancy me? But then I realised I just had to rise above such self-consciousness. I needed to think of these new attachments as being like spectacles, but for the ears rather than the eyes.

Thankfully, hearing loss can never destroy your sense of humour. The story's told that towards the end of his life an increasingly deaf Winston Churchill revisited the House of Commons.

'They say he's potty,' murmured one MP.

Replied Churchill: 'And they say he can't hear either!'

The spiral of violence

My youth was during the Vietnam War era, and I have to confess that as a hawkish young man I found war rather exciting. I remember going to Aberdeen University and seeing a poster that said 'War is not good for children and other living things', and it irritated me for its naivety.

But there were rather a lot of posters like this, and, worked on by my valiant if few-and-far-between girlfriends, I gradually started to think in new ways that chipped away at the armour round my heart.

One of the most influential poster voices was a Brazilian arch-bishop called Hélder Câmara. He'd come out with things like: *'When I give food to the poor, they call me a saint. But when I ask why the poor have no food, they call me a communist.'*

I wonder how many of today's politicians realise that when they are speaking about the 'spiral of violence' in the Middle East, they're drawing on Câmara, who published a little book by that name in 1971.[1]

Câmara observed that violence builds up at three levels in a society. Primary violence is the everyday effect of structurally ingrained social injustice. This generates secondary violence – the revolt of the oppressed. And that in turn provokes tertiary violence – repression by the powerful to secure their privileged position. And so the spiral of violence tightens.

Archbishop Câmara's book culminates with an *'appeal to youth'*, saying that wars happen because of the egotism of adults, and he urges the youth to *'provoke discussions [and] force people to think and take up a position: let it be uncomfortable, like truth, demanding, like justice'*.

Whether in Lebanon or Israel, war is not good for children and other living things, and the children are always innocent. Câmara's last word is for them: 'With you I must remain young in my soul,' he said, 'and keep the hope and love I need to help all humanity.'

Note:

1. Spiral of Violence, Dom Hélder Câmara, Sheed & Ward Ltd, 1971

Spiritual values

It's been a sombre few days as Britain comes to terms with its heaviest military casualties since the Falklands. I find myself looking at the lost men's pictures and seeing, in each one of them, the profound humanity of somebody's son, somebody's father, somebody's lover ...

It might seem strange, but as a Quaker, and therefore an active pacifist, I annually guest lecture at Britain's foremost military staff college.

Over 9 years I've addressed more than 3,000 senior officers. Generally we agree on being willing to die for our values; the debate is whether also to kill for them.

I can tell you that most of these men and women are not warmongers. They, too, see peace as their business. I carry with me a little card that the Army gave me which lists their core values: 'Loyalty, Courage, Integrity, Discipline, Respect for Others and Selfless Commitment'.

These were the values of those the nation grieves for today.

I once asked a general why they let me loose on their campus; and he said, 'You make us think.' It's not rocket science, but I seek to uncover the roots of conflict, and that means exploring how issues like poverty, prejudice and being unloved all feed into wider patterns of violence.

Spirituality then becomes important, because it is about the antidote – about love. In most world religions, love implies that human beings are profoundly interconnected, and that interconnection is the wellspring of community and its regeneration.

That's why I find hope in a conference organised today in Glasgow by Communities Scotland, an agency of the Scottish Executive. Leading politicians and activists are to explore the idea that *spiritual values* can shed fresh light on urban and rural regeneration.

I believe that such innovative thinking at home can have knock-on effects much further afield. I'm left moved by the deaths in Afghanistan this past week, but proud to see Communities Scotland striking a light in the darkness.

The politics we deserve

In the past week Hungary has been rocked by its Prime Minister's disclosure that his party lied to get elected. Meanwhile, our own politicians hammer out policies at their various party conferences, but I have to confess a certain sympathy with the challenges they face in trying to reconcile electoral demands with the ability to deliver.

I'm reminded of one of those stories where a famous politician dies and goes up to the Pearly Gates, only to meet St Peter and the Devil.

St Peter tells him, 'We're going to let you make up your own mind where you go,' and he presses a button so the politician gets to see a preview of himself sitting on a cloud, playing a harp for all eternity.

'Hmmm,' he thinks, '… but it could be a little boring. Maybe I'll just see what the other chap's offering.'

And so the Devil shows him a land of sumptuous restaurants, fabulous theatres and casinos where everyone wins.

The politician's eyes light up, and before he can even speak his thoughts two demons drag him downstairs and hurl him into the Lake of Fire.

Later on the Devil passes by. 'Excuse me,' the politician cries out, 'but I thought you promised sumptuous restaurants, fabulous theatres and –'

'Ah yes,' says the Devil, 'but that's when I was *campaigning*.'

… Of course, it's an old joke; but it's worth asking: why are we so vulnerable to campaigning promises? Is it possible that, like the politician with the Devil, most of us have learned to sit a little too comfortably with lies, because they may seem to comfort us?

If we want our politicians' integrity to be able to shine through, maybe we, the electorate, need to examine our integrity too. Maybe we need to work on building a culture where truth is more the norm.

And that starts not in the realm of national politics, but with the intricate relationships of our everyday lives.

The winds of loss

Another Remembrance Day has passed – yet another grim November's reminder that, for some, the winds of loss forever blow a lonely course. Back in the 1991 war in the Persian Gulf, a BBC reporter put a question to Gabriel Habib, leader of the Middle East Council of Churches.

'Which side of the war is God on?' the reporter asked.

'God,' said Mr Habib, 'is on the side of the suffering.'

With further loss of life on both sides in Iraq, this year's Remembrance Day has left me with a deepening sense of foreboding. Largely gone is the optimism of when the Berlin Wall came down with talk of a 'peace dividend'. Instead, we see renewed nuclear tensions and the fear of terror at many of our airports.

Sometimes it feels as if the world is in the grip of powers greater than our capacity to deal with them. It's as if our humanity itself is being put to the test. Whether it's war or new threats like climate change, it's hard to see ready solutions.

But I am touched by one thing. The Islamic, Jewish and Christian traditions all teach that despair is a sin. We may not have a quick fix, but we can at least kindle an attitude that holds open the doors of hope and dignity. There is only one antidote to despair, and that comes from the human heart. By opening the heart in our daily lives each one of us can play our part.

The French Jesuit priest and scientist Teilhard de Chardin saw such transformation as nothing less than the next step in human evolution. *'Some day... ,'* he wrote, in words that rebuke despair: *'Some day after we have mastered the wind, the waves, the tides, and gravity, we shall harness for God the energies of Love. Then, for the second time in the history of the world, we will have discovered fire.'*

The religion of kindness

This 'Thought' was part of a special Radio Scotland tie-in with Radio Ulster, and was broadcast over both networks.

One of my hats is treasurer to the GalGael Trust, based in Glasgow's shipbuilding area of Govan. Set up by local unemployed people, the GalGael helps folk to reclaim pride in heritage, to discover beauty in the natural environment and to celebrate community.

Over the past decade we've developed training in a vast range of traditional skills: woodcarving, weaving, silversmithing and boatbuilding. Many of our participants received poverty as their birthright, but there's still an inbuilt 'buoyancy of the human soul'[1] that enables even the most damaged human being to bounce back.

Returning from a GalGael day trip recently an adult woman wept in the minibus. Why? Because her childhood dream had just been fulfilled – to see Loch Lomond. But GalGael's most daunting journey was when Down District Council in Ulster invited our crew to the Magnus Barelegs Festival. They crossed the Irish Sea in a boat they'd built from windblown timber out of Glasgow city parks. What a thrill when our 'urban clansmen' beat off even the Northern Irish police rowing team – and sailed triumphantly home with the trophy!

It was exhilarating for them to see the River Clyde opening out into the Irish Sea. For the first time they saw these waters not as a source of division, but as a superhighway that once united our peoples. And what hospitality was shared! As Colin Macleod, GalGael's founder, said, *'We got a real sense of how spirited the ceilidhs must've been when the clans of Ireland and clans of Scotland visited each other by travelling the same route.'*

There's a Celtic proverb that says: *'The bonds of milk are stronger than the bonds of blood.'* What counts most is not our lineage, race or even religion, but whether the milk of human kindness courses in our veins.

Recently I travelled to the Isle of Iona and sat in St Oran's Chapel, where an altar candle shines constantly southwards through a window facing Ireland. In reading Adomnán's seventh-century *Life of Saint Columba*, I noted that our Irish-Scottish missionary had once blessed a pauper for sharing what little he had, but admonished a wealthy miser who, in words Adomnán attributes to Columba, *'had rejected Christ in pilgrim visitors'*.

That's the only religion that can unite us – the religion of kindness. That's what can heal the scars of historic division and it's a sacred gift to us all.

Note:

1. Colin Macleod, founder of the GalGael Trust

A politics of respect

As Alex Salmond became Scotland's First Minister yesterday, Labour's Ewan Aitken of Edinburgh Council spoke of a *'new political reality'* that seeks *'common purpose and agreement'* for the greater good.

But how do you do that? I was in southern Ireland last week and it was amazing to see the warmth with which their press hailed Mr Paisley as 'Big Ian'. And I remembered how, six years ago, my wife and I had taken our students of human ecology to Ulster.

After a day on the Garvaghy Road visiting Catholic groups eloquent with hospitality, we went to the Portadown Orange Lodge.

The atmosphere there was awkward. It was difficult for our

contemporary students to grasp the religious world view of the two senior Orangemen who had generously given up their evening. But then a historical key turned.

'You know, folks,' I said. 'Our hosts are rooted in John Calvin's *Institutes of the Christian Religion* – a book described as *"the seedbed of democracy"*. Whether we agree or not, these men understand Presbyterianism as the root of political freedoms that we now all take for granted.'

It was like an emotional dam burst open. The Orangemen smiled and stretched out their legs. We even ventured a joke, asking how come such resolute egalitarians have such fancy titles as Grand Masters of grand lodges … and everybody laughed.

They could sense that we were now recognising their humanity, and not just seeing them as caricatures.

And that's what a politics of respect does. It gets to the heart of the matter through engaging with the heart. It challenges, yet honours that which is great in the other.

As a Quaker, I move with a spiritual tradition that has done consensual decision-making for nearly four centuries. What makes it work is *discernment* – reaching beyond ego and vested interests for the spirit of truth and right action. You don't try to agree on everything at once, just seek out points of unity from which to build trust. And who knows, if even Gerry Adams and 'Big Ian' can achieve such a new politics, hopefully Scotland can too.

Corporate responsibility

Last night BP broke the news that owing, it said, to Westminster procrastination on funding, it is to abandon the pioneering proposed Peterhead power plant. This would have returned waste carbon dioxide back underground, thereby fighting global warming. Over millions of years, the Earth stored up carbon as fossil fuels and limestone. Such geology tamed the climate by creating an atmosphere that supports advanced life. But when we release carbon by burning fuel in power stations, or industrial processes like cement-making, we upset the balance of nature.

BP say they're disappointed, but let me tell you a good-news story from another industry, the cement sector, which accounts for some five percent of total carbon dioxide emissions. Some years ago I was amongst the many Scottish people and organisations that locked horns with Lafarge, the biggest stone and cement company in the world. They wanted a so-called 'superquarry' in the National Scenic Area of South Harris – but we saw them off.

However, for me that wasn't the end. Lafarge came back and said, 'It's all very well to criticise, but on average each person uses ten tonnes of quarry products a year. Will you help us to think about minimising the impact of this?'

We all have to own up to using corporate products in our daily lives, and so I became an uneasy, albeit unpaid, member of their Sustainability Stakeholders Panel that offers environmental advice. And I've watched how they've reduced carbon dioxide emissions by 14% per tonne of cement from 1990 levels.[1]

I have to admit that my 'auld enemy' has earned some grudging respect. This week they even became the only construction materials company to achieve a top forty FTSE4Good listing by the *Financial Times* for best European environmental practice. That won't save the world, but it's better than doing nothing, and it forces competitors to wake up.

Frankly, I despair at decisions like abandoning the Peterhead power plant. But when I do see financial resources being mobilised for change, as with the cement industry, it at least gives a glimmer of hope for the human condition.

Note:

1. For reports on my terms of reference and engagement with the Lafarge panel: www.alastairmcintosh.com/general/quarry/lafarge-panel.htm

The People's Free Republic of Eigg

In a couple of minutes I'll be leaving Glasgow and heading north for celebrations on the Isle of Eigg. It's exactly a decade since seven generations of landlordism there came to an end. Ten thousand donations from around the world brought the island into community ownership, and a sea change rolled in to Scotland.

I vividly remember how a journalist asked a farmer's wife what it felt like. 'Yesterday,' she replied, 'I had a house, but today, I have a home.'

And for me, that sums up the importance of Scotland's land reform. It deepens people's sense of belonging. It gives folk something to take responsibility for, and that stimulates businesses, social housing and nature conservation – all of which strengthen a sense of community.

Ten years ago in a marquee pitched symbolically on the ex-laird's tennis court, Brian Wilson, then an MP, got up and declared: *'Game set and match to the people of Eigg!'* He also announced the setting up of the Community Land Unit within Highlands and Islands Enterprise. So far this has helped over 150 communities to bring a third of a million acres under their control – and that's an amazing two percent of the entire Scottish land mass!

But as Eigg celebrates, let's also remember Scotland's pioneering Victorian land reformers – Mary MacPherson, John Murdoch and the Reverend Donald MacCallum, to name but three.

They understood that land is about more than just agriculture or economics. It's also a bond that is psychological, cultural and even spiritual. As the Bible puts it, *'The profit of the earth is for all'*[1]; and, as Dougie MacLean sings, *'You cannot own the land. The land owns you.'*[2]

That's the historical character of Scotland's land reform, and I do believe we need that spiritual depth just as much for the future – or else, quite literally, we'd risk – losing the plot.

Notes:

1. Ecclesiastes 5:9, King James (Authorised) Version

2. From the song 'Solid Ground', on *Real Estate*, Dougie MacLean, Dunkeld Records, 1988, www.dougiemaclean.com

'Living for the soul'

There's a passage near the end of Tolstoy's *Anna Karenina* where the hero, Levin, meets a peasant, who contrasts two different types of men.

One type 'just stuffs his belly' and 'lives for his own needs'. The other 'lives for the soul' because, the peasant says, he 'remembers God'.

'How's that?' asks Levin, who's searching for the meaning of life.

'Everybody knows how,' replies the peasant. 'By the truth, by God's way.'[1]

And as Levin takes his leave the peasant's words take root in him. He senses that this honest insistence on truth challenges worldly wisdom. The reasoning powers of the world are often proud and even stupid precisely because they render truth negotiable.

This past week the BBC launched an inquiry into fake phone-in competition results. The Director General said something very interesting. He said, *'A group of people has taken it upon themselves to keep the programme on the air by what they might have regarded at the time as a white lie'* – and he went on to condemn such behaviour as totally unacceptable.[2]

Yet, it's not difficult to understand how easy it must have been for hard-pressed staff to take shortcuts. We all live in a society where so-called 'little white lies' often lubricate social reality. Lying is almost normalised, as when the secretary says that the boss is 'out' when they're simply busy. And yet, each little white lie distorts the surrounding social fabric. That's the problem – the 'little' is deceptive because it panders to a fear of telling the truth.

The stushie at the BBC is bigger than just the misdeeds of a few employees or sub-contractors. It's about us – all of us – and the world we live in. Maybe every one of us who has told white lies needs to own a share in the BBC's embarrassment. Compromising truth is a slippery slope. As Tolstoy's Levin discovered, there is no alternative; none but '*living for the soul, by the truth*'.

Notes:

1. *Anna Karenina*, Penguin Classics, translated by Richard Pevear & Larissa Volokhonsky, 2001, Part 8, Chapter XI

2. www.bbc.co.uk/pressoffice/pressreleases/stories/2007/07_july/19/email.shtml

The parable of the grocer's van

Good morning ... and if I might try saying it in the Gaelic, *Madainn mhath* ... because my attention was caught this week by a story from the Isle of Lewis – about something that used to be totally ordinary: a mobile grocery shop.

It seems that after 44 years on the road, Murdo and Norman Macleod have finally decided to retire from rising early every morning to take essential supplies round the villages.

And essential they certainly were! There were several such vans in business when I was a boy growing up in Lewis, and I well remember the excitement when one would stop near Leurbost School – and we'd all run out for penny toffees and gobstoppers.

We'd fidget in the queue as the driver made sure that every housewife wanting tea or bacon, and every old *bodach* after his tin of tobacco, was properly given the time of day in passing on the island's news.

This was no depersonalised retail therapy of mass consumerism. Instead, these grocery vans embodied the flesh-and-blood relationships of real people in a real place who knew the secret of finding happiness in service to one another.

That's why the retiring van driver, Norman Macleod, could say this week that he'd loved his work, and had a great relationship with his customers because, as he told the press, *They are the greatest people on earth.'*

We live in an era of brash celebrity where bigger is better. The arts of marketing may fill our lives with things, but they can never give us one another.

What so touched me in this Parable of the Grocer's Van was the honest-to-God dignity of ordinary people doing ordinary jobs but with an extraordinary attitude. That's what transforms the commonplace. And that's the love that infuses the sacred into everyday life.

The prophet Micah said this doesn't take rocket science. *'Here is what the Lord requires of you,'* he said: *'to act justly, and to love kindness, and to walk humbly with your God.'*

The spiritual power of witness

The continuing crisis in Burma has dropped off our front pages recently, but the protests seem to have had some effect. In a remarkable development last week, Aung San Suu Kyi, the pro-democracy leader, was shown on state television meeting with a government minister. This Thursday the City of Glasgow is expected to confer its Freedom upon her, and individuals have also strikingly expressed their solidarity.

A month ago I was contacted by an Edinburgh teacher by the name of Ewen Hardie. He's a former student of mine and he'd been shaken by the events unfolding in Burma. Ever since I've know Ewen he'd worn dreadlocks. But now, as an act of witness in solidarity with the monks who are being persecuted, he'd shaved them off. What's more, he'd discarded his shoes, and pledged to carry on bald and barefoot until either it threatens his health or democracy comes to Burma.[1]

Last week the story was picked up on by an Edinburgh newspaper.[2] It has one of those websites where readers post their comments. Some people dismissed Ewen's protest as *completely pointless* – *'a disgrace'* that sets *'a very bad example … to the youngsters'* at his school. The youngsters themselves seemed to think otherwise, and somebody drew parallels with Gandhi, pointing out that *'personal sacrifice lies at the heart of all successful civil rights campaigns'*.

But most telling of all was a response by Aung Naing, a Burmese refugee in Sydney who suffered under the dictatorship.

He said, *'I would like to mention my great thanks to Mr Hardie on behalf of Burmese pro-democracy ordinary people, regardless of how long he can hold his pledge … It impacts a great support to the people who are … imprisoned and tortured in this moment.'*[3]

Violence works by torture, fear and killing. But nonviolence is the power of love that comes from courage in the heart. We might dismiss the monks in Burma, Ewen Hardie in Edinburgh and even the city councillors of Glasgow as hopeless dreamers. But if we do, it is the spiritual power of witness in solidarity that we dismiss, and without that, there would be no hope for freedom.

Notes:

1. www.barefeetforburma.blogspot.co.uk

2. 'City teacher in barefoot Burma protest', 26th October, 2007: www.edinburghnews.scotsman.com/news/city-teacher-in-barefoot-burma-protest-1-1345955

3. From a campaign blog

Burns and Saint Bride

Well, the long dark nights have arrived, and as nature settles to rest so we, too, have the opportunity to shift from outer busyness and rekindle our inner lives.

Our ancient forebears held their bardic schools and ceilidhs during winter. They knew that poetry and music inspires the people and renews the community. That's why I'm thrilled that Scotland is to mark the next two months as a Winter Festival. It starts this Friday on St Andrew's Day and finishes with Burns season at the end of January – which, of course, brings it up to St Bride's or Brigid's Eve, and the symbolism of the returning of the light and spring's new hope.

When announcing the Winter Festival, First Minister, Alex Salmond, spoke of St Andrew's Day as '*a chance to enjoy the multi-cultural Scotland we have become*'.

So what does St Andrew stand for? If we accept the biblical version, he must have been into people's wellbeing, for he played a pivotal role in feeding the five thousand. He also arranged for visiting Greeks to meet with Jesus, which suggests interfaith dialogue.

The idea that Andrew died on an X-shaped cross comes from early Christian traditions. These say he was put to death for persuading Roman soldiers to disarm; and for helping a woman to say 'no' to repeated sexual exploitation by her drunken husband.

We can dismiss these stories, but if we do, we lose the spiritual importance that Andrew, the 'fisher of men', still holds for a modern nation. For me, his saltire symbolises the sharing of plenty, welcome to the stranger, nonviolence, the rights of women … and now, dare I say it, the start of a Winter Festival that squeezes every last drop out of Rabbie Burns' revelry until St

Bride returns the light of spring in the turning of the seasons once again.

Note:

For sources, see: 'Saint Andrew: non-violence & national identity', Alastair McIntosh, *Theology in Scotland*, 2000, p.55

Shall ne'er be truly blest

The BBC website has a page that tells you which news stories get the most hits, and top of the league on Tuesday was one with the heading 'Cruel' Taxi Fare Dodger Hunted.[1]

Seemingly, a guy with a Scottish accent had got into a Newcastle cab and gone all the way to central Scotland. It was the festive season and the driver trusted the customer's sob story that he'd be able to get the £200 fare on arrival, but instead the man ran off.

As Inspector Paul Fleming of Central Scotland Police said: *'This was a cruel act to play on somebody who was trying to make an honest living and who is now considerably out of pocket.'*

As cruel acts go it's hardly in the big-time league. It was a commonplace con, yet it sparked many people's indignation. It certainly did so mine, and for two reasons:

First, as Inspector Fleming said: it's the meanness of cheating a person who serves society through an honest job. But on top of that, here we are in Burns Week. We're celebrating Scotland's generosity of spirit and somebody amongst our number has given a trusting English cabbie cause to think the worst of us!

It damages the reputation of the Scottish people, and as Robert Burns said in his Paraphrase of the First Psalm:

For why? that God the good adore,
Hath giv'n them peace and rest,
But hath decreed that wicked men
Shall ne'er be truly blest.

Well, it's no good just moaning about insults to the national dignity but whenever I hear a story like this it really rankles me. I'll tell you what I'm going to do. I get a modest fee for presenting *Thought for the Day*. It's only a fraction of the unpaid taxi fare, but today that's being offered to the cheated driver from Newcastle. It might at least buy him a good dram when he comes off-duty ... and may the spirit of Robert Burns endure, for with it Scotland is truly blest.

Note:

1. 'Cruel' Taxi Fare Dodger Hunted, BBC News, Tuesday, 22 January 2008: http://news.bbc.co.uk/1/hi/scotland/tayside_and_central/7201996.stm

What God gets

It must have been disturbing for people on that Air Canada flight to Heathrow this week when the co-pilot had to be restrained by his colleagues and forced off the flight deck while yelling out that he wanted to ... *'speak to God'*. Apparently he's now in a psychiatric hospital, with his wife looking after him; and the airline has responded in a very level-headed way, saying that: *'The captain and crew followed correct operational procedures when the co-pilot fell ill.'*[1]

Well, that's all very reassuring, but the story raises wider questions about religion, questions that account for the fervid headlines in many of the hundred and eighty-three newspaper reports of what happened that can be found on the Internet. You can just imagine Professor Richard Dawkins rubbing his hands at yet another crazy case study of what he calls *'the God delusion'*. And it was the philosopher Bertrand Russell who said that, from a scientific point of view, we can make no distinction between the man who drinks much and sees snakes, and the one who eats little and sees God.

Indeed, God gets a bad press, and there's maybe a good reason for that. As I once heard a priest say, *'God gets what man rejects.'* God gets the poor, the broken, the lonely hearts and the mentally ill. None of that belittles the seriousness of what happened on Air Canada Flight 848. But it does raise the consideration that if people are at their wits' end, then maybe it's not surprising if they issue the Mayday call of last recourse and send out an SOS to the ground of their deepest being.

This morning a Canadian airline pilot is under recovery, and God, yet again, is back in the dock. What's your verdict going to be? Are you going to condemn God? Or will you, like God, send out your heart in solidarity with those who suffer?

Note:

1.www.dailymail.co.uk/news/article-511220/This-pilot-speaking—crying-swearing-And-demanding-talk-God.html

Fishers of men

In Aberdeen tomorrow there's going to be a gathering of some fifty organisations concerned about the state of Scotland's fishing communities. Fishing means a lot to me. When I was a boy on Lewis, the old men would take us out in their boats. We'd let down hand lines baited with mussels and usually pull in a good haul of 'haddies' and whiting. As we shared them out in the village we learned the meaning of community. It was a well-mentored rite of passage for us young men into the responsibilities of adult life.

But much of that came to an end in the 1970s. Technical developments and political trade-offs changed fishing from a way of life to a capital-intensive industry. The resource was steadily ruined and fishing communities died from within.

Tomorrow's conference has been organised by the Economic and Social Research Council. It aims to help the Scottish government explore ways of rekindling fishing communities. Past polices have treated fishing just like any other industry. But it's not just another industry. It's a whole way of life based on the relationship between people and a wild natural resource. It's about community in the fullest sense because it integrates marine biology with economics, culture and even spirituality. Fishing teaches us that everything is interconnected. You can't pull on just one loop of a tangled hand line without finding it joined to all the other loops.

The Aberdeen conference will report back to St Andrew's House, the HQ of the Scottish Office. The outer doors of that building bear an inscription. It says, *'And I will make you fishers of men.'* And there's the answer to saving Scotland's fishing communities. It needs to be about people, and their being empowered to take responsibility for their own resources. In other words, it's like land reform, but for the sea.

The parable of the northern seed

There's been a lot recently about road equivalent tariffs that will further subsidise ferries to the Outer Hebrides. I think it's wonderful, but it's expensive, and therefore raises an old question about give and take between Scotland's urban centre and its rural periphery.

One answer to the question struck me last September. I was at the John Lennon Northern Lights Festival in Durness – Scotland's most northerly village – where Lennon used to spend family holidays.

In a field by the hotel where the bands were playing there was an old crofter who was making stooks from his harvest of oats. I watched as loads of people stopped and he generously gave them all the time of day.

I, too, paused with a question. Did he think that the 'improved' modern strains are as hardy as the oats we traditionally grew?

'Not at all,' he replied. 'Most modern varieties are bred in the south. But we used to bring our seed down from Orkney. That way it worked for our conditions.'

And then he added something. He said: 'We used to say: *the seed must move from north to south.*'

I walked away feeling like I'd just been given 'The Parable of the Northern Seed'.

It's true – the economic powerhouse of the Central Belt does subsidise remote parts of rural Scotland.

But then you look at all those visitors to the north, mainly from the south, and you see that, like John Lennon, they go back uplifted by the spirit of the place to which they've been.

As such, the hidden exports of remote areas – whether in the north or elsewhere – are cultural and spiritual qualities. Alongside economic wealth, these are what provide social cohesion and a welcome to the stranger. These are what bind us as nation, where the things that count are more than just what can be counted. And that, it seems to me, is the Parable of the Northern Seed.

Idolatry of consumerism

I'm talking today from the BBC's Belfast studio. I'm here to discuss climate change, and whether religion can help to tackle it.

Later this morning a cross-section of faith leaders will be sitting down at the invitation of Friends of the Earth in Northern Ireland.

Even as they gather, the official death toll from the cyclone in Burma will be rising by the hour. Over 22,000 are now confirmed dead and the British Ambassador estimates that the final figure may be nearer 50,000.

We must be careful not to suggest that the Burmese tragedy was caused by climate change. Natural disasters always happen. But most informed scientists believe that extreme weather events are likely to get more frequent because of global warming. It's the same as heating a saucepan – the more you turn it up, the more it blows off steam and boils over.

So what can the world's religions do about this? I'll tell you what I'll be saying this morning.

Most experts consider that global warming is mainly caused by human impact on the environment. The relatively rich trash the planet, and the poor, living in vulnerable places, are most likely to suffer the consequences.

That makes climate an ethical issue, which is why it's relevant to religion. Human impact on the earth is driven not just by necessary *consumption*, but also by unnecessary *consumerism*.

The power of marketing has misled many people into thinking that fulfilment comes not from who we are, but from what we have.

In religious language, that's idolatry. It pulls us away from life's chief end and fobs us off with things that can never last.

That's what makes climate change a spiritual issue. We need to balance our outer lives with a rekindled inner life.

It's not just the outer climate that needs attention – it's the inner one too.

Commonplace honesty

On Monday a major report was published on the future of Scottish crofting. Yesterday Mike Russell, the Environment Minister, said that *'radical change is needed to reverse years of decline'*, and happily this seems to be a cross-party consensus.

When I leave this studio shortly I'll be jumping on a train to Inverness where, this afternoon, the Scottish Crofting Foundation and the University of the Highlands and Islands will be taking matters further. They'll be asking whether crofters merit the same special cultural status as indigenous peoples elsewhere in the world.

That actually raises a question about the identities of all Scots. What kind of a people are we, and what values signify who we are?

Now, I have to travel a lot in my work, and regular listeners may remember that last week it meant presenting *Thought for the Day* from Belfast. I don't know what it sounded like at your end, but I can tell you, I wasn't at my best!

The previous evening I'd left my Filofax in the Wetherspoon's bar at Glasgow Airport. It had nearly a hundred pounds in it, my credit cards, driving licence and diary.

As you might imagine, I didn't sleep too well that night, and I could have done without having to set off for the BBC studio at the crack of dawn.

But to my relief, once back at Glasgow Airport's lost property office, I found that an honest waiter had done the decent thing. And I asked the woman behind the desk how often such valuables are recovered.

'Oh, you'd be amazed,' she told me. 'Nearly everything gets handed in. There's a lot more honest people out there than you'd imagine.'

And so, back to this afternoon's crofting seminar and the question: What kind of a people are we, and what values do we hold in common?

It's easy to open the newspapers and to think that society's gone to the dogs. But I can tell you, when I got my Filofax back and learned that such honesty is normal, I felt proud of the values of the Scottish people.

Jesus saves

A report from Scottish Widows in the news yesterday reveals that a third of us are not paying sufficient into pension schemes for a comfortable life after work.

Those saving enough are – wait for it – most likely to be male, over 50, and earning at least thirty thousand.

Ever since Thatcherism upped the ante in privatising the provision for old age I've found something profoundly disturbing about this idea that we can buy future security by placing faith in Mammon – the god of money.

I happen to have a Financial MBA so I know it's all very logical. And we nearly all dabble in it to varying degrees. And when it's just the way the world's gone, there may not seem to be much choice.

But ultimately we have to ask how best to provide for our security in old age. Do we all have our own little stash hoarded away? Or do we try to build a social community that accepts being our neighbour's keeper?

Why can't those of us working now simply pay enough tax to support the present generation of pensioners and then be looked after in our turn? Why not cut out much of the bloated financial system? Do we really trust it more than we trust one another?

After all, money is simply the power to take a bigger slice of the common cake. Globally it's not going to protect us from energy shortages or climate change driving up food prices.

Long ago a crazy man called John the Baptist said, 'Whoever has two shirts must share with who has none, and anyone who has food must do the same.'[1]

And John's best friend warned against seeking security in gold and possessions. Both men placed their investments in the community. And as far as we know, that best friend, whose name was Jesus, never saved ... in a bank.

Note:

1. Luke 3:11 (Common English Bible)

Sacred marriage

Summertime is here, and with it the season of weddings. Scotland is one of just six countries where humanist weddings are legally recognised, and figures just out show that these were up by sixty-four percent to seven hundred and ten last year.

Most humanists believe that rationality should be the factor that determines our human affairs. As such, they say that we don't need spirituality, and we can do most decisively without 'God'!

I respect that view, yet I can't help wondering if it misses something.

Marriage poses fundamental questions about what it really means to be in profound relationship with another human being. You may, like Bertrand Russell, think we're no more than what he called *'the outcome of accidental collocations of atoms'*[1] – here today and gone tomorrow.

But what grabs me more is all those songs about true love being 'forever and a day', or, as Rabbie Burns put it, lasting *'till a' the seas gang dry ... and the rocks melt wi' the sun!'* [2]

These hint that we're only partly of the material world. Our greater selves connect beyond space and time, uniting us as members one of another, like the branches of a tree sprung from a taproot in eternity.

And so, while I'm glad that Scotland can honour the rich diversity that includes humanism, I'd also want to say that, for me, there's been times when God, or whatever name we want to call it by, has shone out like a shaft of light through dark clouds.

That leaves me wondering if the poets might have got it right. It raises the possibility that marriage is not just about working things through in the material world. One foot for sure belongs in the here and now. But I believe the other foot reaches out to the source of our deepest longing, and that's the point where love meets eternity.

Notes:

1. From *The Basic Writings of Bertrand Russell*, George Allen & Unwin Ltd, London, 1961, p.39

2. From 'My love is like a red, red rose'

A footballing legend

It's the time of year when school-leavers are thinking about what to make of their exam results. Yesterday when buying my morning paper I was talking to a young Scot whose parents came here from Pakistan and who's presently wondering how best he can serve the family business. Is it by helping his dad from behind the counter, or should he go and study accountancy so that he can also do the books?

You know what it's like at that age. It's hard to see the wider picture of what your life might become. Mick Jagger once said he'd sooner die than still be playing 'Satisfaction' at forty, but for many of us, the Great Cosmic Conveyer Belt of Life long since passed forty and still hasn't run into the buffers.

That's when you start weighing up where you're at now in relation to how you saw yourself away back then.

And that's also what I find so interesting about obituaries in the newspapers. A good obituary lets you see somebody's life as a completed work of art.

Although I live within hearing distance of Ibrox, I happen to have no interest whatsoever in football. And yet when I read my paper yesterday I delighted in an obituary for Bob Crampsey, described as *'a gentleman, a scholar ... and a Scottish footballing legend'.*[1]

Here was a man who had become a priceless work of Scottish art. Here was a role model whose life combined not just a passion for sport, but also wide-ranging learning and the qualities of a thoroughly decent human being.

I don't believe that success in life is about what you possess or how much you earn. But I do think it's about making choices that allow the unfolding of all-round potential. That's what a good Scots education has always aspired towards, that's the richer meaning of wealth, and at the end that's what allows others to look back and give thanks for a life fulfilled.

Note:

1. www.heraldscotland.com/a-gentlemen-a-scholar-and-a-scottish-footballing-legend-1.885516

Whatever it takes

This month has been a critical one in the history of our nation, one that historians will look back on as marking a cultural watershed.

Our faith in money has been shaken and earlier this week Gordon Brown promised a *'central mission'* of doing *'whatever it takes'* to spend a way out of the economic black hole.[1]

At the same time, and almost lost amongst the economic headlines, the UK government took a courageous step towards tackling dangerous climate change. It now matches Scotland's aspiration by having raised from 60 percent to 80 percent the target for cutting greenhouse gas emissions by the year 2050.

But setting targets is the easy bit; achieving them is harder. And there's the rub. Both the economic bubble now bursting and global warming have one driver in common: consumerism. Our conundrum is that we need more consumption to save the economy, but less to save the planet.

Spending our way out of a recession is therefore only a stopgap measure. It's methadone for our planetary heroin addiction.

We simply feed the habit if we think that today's problems can be tackled at conventional political, technical or economic levels. If we're redefining our *'central mission'*, we must press further.

Technical fixes are certainly part of the solution. But I'd put it to you that the deep work must be this: to learn to live more abundantly with less, to rekindle community, and to serve fundamental human need instead of worshiping at the altars of greed.

The crisis of these times is therefore spiritual. It calls for reconnecting our inner lives with the outer world – an expansion of consciousness. And that's an opportunity that we neglect at our peril, for, as I once heard an old Quaker woman say, 'It is perilous to neglect one's spiritual life.'

Note:

1. www.heraldscotland.com/pm-vows-uk-will-spend-its-way-out-of-recession-despite-debt-1.892583

Faith in money

Yesterday vandals attacked the home of Sir Fred Goodwin, former boss of the Royal Bank of Scotland, and meanwhile, caught in the economic tidal wave, the Dunfermline Building Society is having to reach out for a government lifeline.

These two institutions have a different basis. The Royal Bank exists to maximise profit for shareholders. The Dunfermline, on the other hand, is a mutual society. It seeks no profit beyond running costs to link up savers and borrowers.

Put like that it's easy to point the finger at banks like the Royal and 'Fred the Shred' for having played casino with our money. But let's remember, most people never questioned matters when their house prices and pension portfolios kept rising. Silence was the voice of complicity.

Money works only if we have confidence in it. That word, *confidence*, comes from the Latin *con-fidere*, meaning *'to have faith together'*. The canonisation of greed undermines that faith. It worships a false god that ultimately betrays our society.

All three of the Abrahamic religions accept money's primary role of being an IOU system, but they challenge what economists recognise as its secondary role of making money out of money by charging compound interest. Today usury usually means the practice of lending money at excessive rates of interest, but originally it meant any form of return that insulated the lender from the welfare of the borrower.

Jewish law banned usury within its own community. Jesus urged lending without the expectation of getting a return. And Islam condemns the charging of interest because, in the words of the Qur'an, it *'devour[s] men's substance wrongfully'.*[1]

Next month the G20 leaders of the world meet in London. Will they simply re-spin the casino economy's roulette wheel? Or might they consider a more mutual basis for wellbeing? We shall be watching, for where a politician's heart is, so our money follows.

Notes:

1. Scriptural references: Exodus 22:25, Luke 6:35, Qur'an 4:161

For background on the history of usury prohibition, see my paper with Wayne Visser: www.alastairmcintosh.com/articles/1998_usury.htm

Without vision

I've just read a remarkable new report with the challenging title of *Prosperity without Growth?*[1] The report, on the UK government's Sustainable Development Commission website, argues that more and more economic expansion cannot fix the problems of the world: that *'the myth of growth has failed us'.*

Instead of cultivating human qualities like trust, love and community, we've tried to buy the stairway to heaven. Consumerism is therefore at the cutting edge of both the short-term credit crunch and the long-term crunch of climate change.

The world economy would need to expand by fifteen times for everybody to catch up on our level of materialism by 2050. But the earth already can't afford the profligacy of the rich, so what can we do? And how can the poor at home and abroad get their fair share?

This week saw heart-warming inspiration from Provost Bill Howatson of Aberdeenshire Council. Instead of choosing to be driven on official duties in a Jaguar, a Bentley, or a Daimler, he's opted for a fifty-five-miles-to-the-gallon Skoda.

Asked if the status loss bothered him, he replied that he was *'pleased to be seen in an environmentally friendly car that will be more economical to run and cheaper to purchase. It reflects the vision of the Council.'* [2]

And there's the nub. A biblical proverb reminds us that *'Where there is no vision, the people perish.'* [3] The vision needed to tackle consumerism is voluntary simplicity like that taken on here by Provost Howatson.

What's needed now is a mindset shift for us all. We need to drop our admiration of the grandiose and maybe even start seeing fancy status symbols as badges of shame and insecurity.

The *Prosperity without Growth?* report calls for *'underlying human values'* and a seeking of *'the common good'*. When I get to see the Aberdeenshire Provost's new car, that's what I'll be admiring.

Notes:

1. *Prosperity without Growth?: the Transition to a Sustainable Economy*, Professor Tim Jackson, Sustainable Development Commission, 2009

2. www.scotsman.com/news/scotland/top-stories/provost-lords-it-up-in-a-skoda-1-1033337

3. Proverbs 29:18, KJV

You'll have had your comfort

As we take stock of the mind-boggling sums being spent on bailing out the nation's economy, many must be wondering who's going to pay. Will it be those who stuffed their pockets in the boom-time years? Or might the axe fall upon the poor?

That question will be with me this evening when I go to an event in Easterhouse in Glasgow. An old friend, the poverty campaigner Cathy McCormack, is launching her autobiography. It's called *The Wee Yellow Butterfly*,[1] and the title is connected to something that happened to her in a community workshop.

She'd been told to imagine being a caterpillar ... transforming into a butterfly. But Cathy thought: *Butterfly? What chance have I to become a butterfly? ...*

She'd spent twenty years fighting official indifference to damp and mould-ridden housing in her community.

But then, finally, her work started achieving recognition, and she was sent on a fact-finding visit to Nicaragua.

It was here that she became inspired by liberation theology: the idea that God is on the side of the poor – but that God has been misrepresented by the rich to keep the poor down, while the wealth gets creamed off.

We're talking here of biblical passages about which few sermons are preached, like Luke 6, where Jesus says: *'Woe to you who are rich ... for you have had your comfort.'*[2] Or as Islam puts it: *'He who eats and drinks whilst his brother goes hungry is not one of us.'*[3]

But far from writing off the rich, liberation theology is about their humanity: found by entering into solidarity with the poor. As Gustavo Gutiérrez, the Peruvian father of the movement, who spoke in Stirling in 1995, has said: 'to liberate means *to give life'.*

Notes:

1. *The Wee Yellow Butterfly*, Cathy McCormack with Marian Pallister, Argyll Publishing, 2009

2. Luke 6:24

3. Hadith of al-Bukhari (pbuh)

The Hebridean Sabbath

I've just come back from a 12-day walk in the Hebrides – what I jokingly called a 'poacher's pilgrimage' on account of the fishing rod I took with me while traversing mountain passes and remote glens.

The less said about the fishing the better, but I had a rich time exploring ancient sheilings on the moors, drinking from long-since venerated wells, and pausing at both pre-Reformation and modern Presbyterian centres of worship, which stretch from the southern tip of Harris to the Butt of Lewis.

Friend and stranger alike invited me into their homes. Never would I leave without a full belly or a newly laid clutch of eggs. Not having seen the newspapers I'd ask what was fresh. The General Assembly was dominating national news, but the burning local issue was the renewed threat of Sabbath ferry sailings to Stornoway.

While opinions are sharply divided, a great many people, including the local authority, are staunchly opposed. It's a marker of cultural identity as well as a religious issue; one that ought not to be imposed from afar, but decided through the settled will of the local community.

Personally I'm not a rigid Sabbatarian, yet having been raised on Lewis I do find myself touched by some of what radiates from the Hebridean lighthouse. As a self-employed writer and academic

I've got choice over my use of time. But the concern on Lewis is for the impact that delivery lorry and tourist arrivals would have on low-paid service workers. For these, not having to work on Sundays is a form of employment protection that safeguards family and community life.

We live in strange times, and since the credit crunch meltdown many are starting to question the 24/7 hubris of economic life. And so, who knows. Could it be that the Hebridean Sabbath is actually a treasure of cultural diversity that Scotland should cherish?

Maybe there's a baby in that bathwater at risk of being thrown out – and He's not just looking back, but pointing forwards.

Broken millstones

I've just finished reviewing a most beautifully produced volume from a small Stornoway publisher. It's about the Norse mills of Lewis.[1] The ruins of these stone-built corn mills are all around. You see them lining the banks of streams from where they drew water power to grind the oats and barley that were once the mainstay of a self-sufficient way of life.

But those days were numbered. During the eighteenth century, landowners auctioned off the rights to build commercially run mills. Their owners were empowered to break village millstones and thereby force people into a market economy.

I thought about this when I heard Tuesday's news that CalMac, the state-owned ferry company, had suddenly announced Sunday sailings to Stornoway as from this weekend.

To traditionalists this disables the Hebridean Sabbath's function as a community blessing. It breaks it like a millstone beneath the hammer of 'progress'.

If such change was clearly the settled will of the community, then so be it. But at present the question is very far from settled. The local authority is strongly opposed to the sailings, though some councillors are probably divided between their private views and political necessity. And amongst island opinion generally, there are many with principled positions on both sides, and for that matter, each side can count both secular and religious supporters.

As the mills of God grind slowly on, one thing for the record is sure. It has never been the island's clearly expressed wish that this ancient stone be broken.

Far from being a quaint Hebridean custom, it touches on something we maybe all need for the rhythm of the working week to be punctuated by a time of togetherness.

And in that stilling of the world's outer clamour, a space within to listen. For how else can we hope to hear the Spirit's voice?

Notes:

1. Reviewed in the *Stornoway Gazette.* Copy of the review at: www.alastairmcintosh.com/articles/2009-Norse-Mills-Review.htm

Finlay MacLeod (Fionnlagh MacLeòid) has published two versions of this book: in English, *The Norse Mills of Lewis*, Mills Archive Trust, and, in Gaelic, *Muilnean Beaga Leòdhais*, Acair Ltd, Stornoway

When the ferries fail to sail

It's a year ago today since our banking systems were very nearly engulfed following the collapse of Lehman Brothers in America. And I bet I'm not alone in wondering *what if* our own government's financial bailout had not happened.

Not only might the hole-in-the-wall have stopped talking to us, but our globalised food supply system could also have been thrown into chaos, because without the banks doing their bit you don't get the deliveries coming through.

I've thought a lot about this recently while working with an Edinburgh University student seconded to my supervision. She went up to Stornoway and interviewed people about what happens when the Ullapool ferry fails to sail because of bad weather.[1]

She learned that the supermarket shelves quickly go bare, and not just because of panic buying. It's also because restocking is on a just-in-time basis, and so there's no slack to make up for any disruption in the system.

For the sake of comparison she then went on to interview people who could remember the six-week-long seamen's strike in 1966 which forced Harold Wilson to declare a national state of emergency.

Most people said they'd avoided hardship because crofting was still vibrant. They had their own potatoes, hens, sheep, and maybe a cow for milk or a fishing boat moored in the loch. But above all, they had an ethos of sharing.

This gave the local economy the resilience by which it could stand up to knocks. In contrast, today we have greater efficiency, but it's also a more brittle system – which the banking crisis very nearly taught us.

The lesson is that economic efficiency is vital, but only if matched by the community resilience that makes for true security.

That's why such examples as Fair Trade, farmers' markets and local entrepreneurship are all so important.

They remind us that the economy should be not just about money, but also about the human handshakes that reflect right relationships ... for they're what counts when the ferry fails to sail.

Note:

1. Lauren Eden and Alastair McIntosh, 'When the Ferries Fail to Sail', *Dark Mountain*, Issue 5, April 2014

The joy of sex

I was surprised how pleased I was this week to learn that Holyrood's Justice Committee has agreed to investigate the display of soft pornography on newsagent stands.

Surprised, because I'm deeply grateful for having been a child of the sixties when, at last, sex was liberated from the straitjacket of the upright and uptight.

As the poet Philip Larkin famously said: *'Sexual intercourse began in 1963 (which was rather late for me) - Between the end of the Chatterley ban and the Beatles' first LP'*[1] – and that was followed over the next decade by books like *The Joy of Sex*, which completed many of our educations!

So, why do I feel affronted when, like yesterday, I go into a railway newsagent and see a daily paper in full view – its front page showing a young woman in underwear, bent over in the most provocative posture? I asked the sales manager about it. He said the female staff especially don't like it, but it's company policy to stock the publications.

What is it, then, that distinguishes the joy of sex from mere obscenity?

This week happens to be Quaker Awareness Week, so let me tell you how Quakers saw it back when the sexual revolution was in full swing. They recognised that sex can be destructive or creative, but which way round is determined by the principle that: *'No relationship can be a right one which makes use of another person through selfish desires.'*[2]

And there's the nub, because sex is about physical sensation, but to fulfil it joyfully, and creatively, it must mutually give expression to the heart. And that's what's lacking from pornography, because it uses people for money.

That's why I welcome Holyrood's cross-party investigation of what gets to be normalised on our newsstands. This is about much more than just what children happen to see. This is about 'adult' material that degrades sex itself. It's about our humanity, because that's what pornography defiles.

Notes:

1. From 'Annus Mirabilis', by Philip Larkin

2. *Quaker Faith & Practice*, 22:11

Imaging the infinite

Tomorrow is Advent Sunday in the Christian cycle of marking out the year.

When I was small it meant only one thing – the Advent calendars that my granny would send to me and my sister.

You know what I mean … little windows to open each day in the countdown to Christmas, with a big one at the end that contained a square of chocolate.

By that time, of course, Santa was loading up his sledge – and you'd shortly have enough chocolate to last a week.

And in my child's mind there was no question who came up trumps between Jesus Christ and Father Christmas. Santa was the man who delivered!

You wrote your letter, sent it up the chimney, and the goodies turned up … just in time.

I can still remember the tinge of sadness after starting school when the whispering campaign began, and the magic turned to potato peelings and ashes.

And I kind of sensed that the faerie on the Christmas tree, and gentle Jesus meek and mild might slide the same way too. It was a hardening world.

It took until my own children came along to rehabilitate Father Christmas. The old magic came alive again and I saw that this wasn't about a literal truth. It was part of the spirit of generosity that is Christmas; the magic of story that goes beyond words.

Over the years I've also come to rethink prayer like this. We might be Christians, Buddhists, Jews or people of goodwill with no particular faith. But there's something beyond literal truth that maybe starts with words and child-like images, but which points us to the infinite …

Settle us, in this moment, to that depth within.
Open life's heart to our deepest yearnings.
Show us how to love, and be loved.
Forever.
Amen

Saint Andrew's manliness

Today's the day of Andrew – the patron saint of Scotland. But for some people, men and children – but I'm thinking especially of women – it won't be a happy day to wake up to.

It will be a day of nursing last night's wounds, and in many ways, domestic violence is the most confusing type of assault, because it comes from those supposed to love you.

So what's Saint Andrew's part?

In the Bible he was the first-called of the disciples. He introduced visiting Greeks to Jesus and the lad with the loaves and fishes, but otherwise he doesn't do much.

To appreciate how our distant forebears shaped the making of the saint we have to go back to very early Christian writings, like *The Acts of Andrew*.

These tell how he became the spiritual teacher of Maximilla, wife of the Roman Proconsul, Aegeates. She confided how every night her husband came home drunk and forced himself upon her.

Andrew – whose name means 'manliness' – encouraged her to treat this with zero tolerance.

Aegeates had him flogged, specially tied to an X-shaped cross to prolong the agony, and crucified at Patras.

Here domestic violence links to the ugliness of empire and strikes out far beyond the home. It profoundly distorts a person's sense of what's normal and acceptable.

Recently I listened to a hard-pressed mother telling Scotland's Poverty Truth Commission how she'd gone from an abusive father to a violent husband. She said, *'I was never going to marry anyone who'd be nice to me, because I'd never known anything nice.'*

... Andrew stood by Maximilla, as she broke that spell of violence.

May his gentle manliness be our inspiration.
Let us today remember Andrew.
Patron saint of a woman's right to say 'no'.
Amen

Notes:

The Poverty Truth Commission: www.povertytruthcommission.org

This Radio 4 *Prayer for the Day* reflection was also used by Johann Lamont MSP in a Scottish Parliament debate on domestic violence.

The three eyes

People often ask what spirituality is, and how to open up to it.

One response comes from a medieval mystic called Richard of Saint Victor. For him, spirituality wasn't about imposing belief systems on the world, but about an ever-deepening direct perception of reality.

He said that we have three eyes: The eye of the flesh reveals the physical world. The eye of reason lets us see sense. And then there's the eye of the soul.

That eye is like the other two. If we don't use it, if we don't *look* … then we won't see.

But how is the eye of the soul opened? That's what the spiritual practices of many different paths are about.

I have a morning contemplation that I try to follow.

In my mind's eye, I'll slowly scan up and down my body, becoming present to every physical sensation and especially observing inner pools of emotion.

I'll then shift attention to the coming day's activity. I'll gently look at what's needing done, and see what's most calling out for attention. And sometimes it's at odds with my carefully planned 'To do' list.

Lastly I'll observe how my life's being held in the greater life of this world, and open out to just a few of the people, organisations and issues that I in turn help to hold.

And perhaps I'll hear the Pakistani neighbour scraping off the ice, starting up his grocer's van and setting off in service to the community.

And I'll silently wish him safety, and respect, and in his Islamic custom: *As-Salāmu 'Alaykum.*

… And that's about it really.

… But it feels a kind of blessing.

… And it feels like being blessed.

… Amen

First temptation: power of nature

Straight after Jesus' baptism he heads off to the desert and fasts while being tempted by 'the Devil'.

It's a problematic story to read literally. The gospels don't even agree on the ordering of the temptations. But read as poetic truth some very deep insights open up.

Here we have the metaphorical 'Devil' (from the Greek *diabolos*). A juggler's 'diabolo' is a prop which consists of 'a spool which is whirled and tossed on a string tied to two sticks held one in each hand'.

That's the deeper meaning of *diabolos*: throwing something out across the path of another person's life – traducing them; tripping them up with deception, slander and lies.

So here's the Devil trying to trip Jesus up … and telling him to turn stones into bread is such a seemingly benign and childlike suggestion …

Yet think of its power in a hungry world: precisely the power of industrial agriculture, in which minerals, coal and oil drive intensive food production.

On the one hand such technology can be seen as a blessing. It has enabled nearly seven billion people to inhabit this planet.

On the other hand, it's easy to lose sight of the limits, and so allow wider consumerism to drive climate change – with consequences potentially nothing short of diabolical.

That's why the United Nations will meet in Copenhagen next week to see what more can be done about global climate change.

… Help us to see that this crisis runs deeper than what politics, economics and technology alone can fix: that it's a spiritual crisis too – one of right relationship with the powers of nature.

Help us also to hallow science … where its gifts are used to serve the earth, and not just to make a killing.

Give us this day our daily bread.

Amen

Second temptation: social power

Yesterday I reflected on the first temptation of Christ – to turn stones into bread, and so to abuse the powers of nature.

Today I want to look at the abuse of social power – Christ's second temptation in Saint Luke's ordering of them – and again to read the story not literally, but as metaphor.

So picture the scene: Here's this young man in his early thirties who's been fasting alone in the desert for forty days and forty nights.

Days and nights ... a reminder that we wrestle with life's deepest issues not just in the cold light of rationality, but also in the mythical depths of our unconscious.

Here's Jesus ... embodying our all-so-human vulnerability ... and then, as we might imagine it, with a flash and a bang and a horrible whiff of sulphur ... enter the crusty old Devil.

He offers Jesus all the kingdoms of the world.

Never mind whether he's really got the title deeds! But he waves them all about, flaunting the temptations of political power, landed power and military might.

I wonder: how might I have responded?

Think what happens when an ordinary person suddenly gets extraordinary power. How might we have stumbled but for the grace of God?

There's a Persian proverb that behind every rich man is a devil, but behind every poor man are two.

Everybody sees the devil of another's wealth or power. But when we've never been tested we've got both the devil we know and the one which, given half a chance, might emerge.

We all have to struggle with our demons. We all have to decide where in the great watershed questions of life we're going to stand.

It's rarely black and white, but in the motto of one global company: *'Don't be evil.'*

Amen

Third temptation: spiritual power

I've been looking this week at the temptations of Christ, and we've reached the third where the Devil flies Jesus to the top of the temple and tells him to jump off.

What a stunt! For wouldn't legions of angels come to his rescue?

But Jesus replies: 'Don't put God to the test.' It's the temptation to abuse spiritual power.

We may live in a world that often denies the spiritual, but power denied is power abused, and spiritual abuse cuts to the marrow of the soul.

For me, these three temptations of Christ are challenges to the three pillars of community.

Turning stones to bread breaks community with the environment, abusing nature's power.

To seize kingdoms breaks community with one another, abusing social power.

And to misuse personal charisma breaks community with the divine, abusing spiritual power.

So what might protect us from these temptations? In many traditions the antidotes are poverty, chastity and obedience. Perhaps these loaded words need a fresh eye.

Poverty protects against the abuse of nature; not as hair-shirt self-denial, but as the rich simplicity of a full cup that doesn't need to overflow.

And chastity, which mustn't be confused with celibacy; for chaste friendship is pure friendship forged in honest empathy, whether sexual or not.

Lastly, obedience. Not necessarily to any human authority, but to the calling of our own innermost soul. Like Shakespeare said: *'floating … obedient to the streame'*.[1]

It's what the Chinese call flowing with the Tao. To Hindus it's walking in the Dharma. And to Christians it's blowing in the wind of the Holy Spirit.

… Lead us in such paths of poverty, chastity and obedience.

Amen

Note:

1. *The Comedy of Errors*

Wisdom of the Sadhu

2009 will be remembered for the economic crisis, politicians' expenses, the Afghan war and global extremes in the weather. Even the Queen's Christmas speech suggested it might be a year 'best forgotten'.

And yet, the current wintery conditions have surprisingly had me thinking about hope, prompted by a story that my mother first told me as a boy, when we were travelling in the car from Stornoway.

Such was its impression that I still remember the spot on the road where she told it. But recently, I was thrilled to discover its original source – thanks to a book called *Wisdom of the Sadhu*, about an Indian holy man, Sundar Singh.[1]

Born in the Punjab of a Sikh father and a Hindu mother he was additionally inspired by Islam, Buddhism and Christianity, and even preached in Protestant churches here in Scotland, prior to his death eighty years ago.

Singh's story is that once, when travelling in Tibet, he and a guide got caught in a terrible blizzard. Under bitter conditions they chanced on some poor soul who had slipped from the mountain path and was lying in snow half dead from exposure.

Wrapping him in a blanket, Singh hoisted the man over his shoulders. But the guide wasn't up for being slowed down by passengers, and set off alone to save his own skin.

Singh struggled for hours with his burden, but eventually the snow let up enough for him to see a village and safety ahead. But also on the path was another body – frozen – this time of his guide, who had failed to make it.

Singh realised that he and his companion had survived thanks to the warmth of the physical exertion, and to their sharing of body heat.

This evening, as we leave behind the old year, we too will face burdens on the path.

But as Sadhu Sundar Singh showed, the secret is to transform them in a greater vision, and practice, of becoming more fully human.

Then may this New Year be truly happy.

Note:

1. *Wisdom of the Sadhu: Teachings of Sundar Singh*, Sadhu Sundar Singh, Plough Publishing House, 2000

A dry Burns supper

I've been thinking this week about how we celebrate Robert Burns and Burns Night.

The significance hit me the other evening at the Burns Supper of the GalGael Trust, a Govan-based organisation that I'm involved with. It's best known for building and sailing traditional boats down the Clyde, but our deeper work is about people – tackling unemployment, broken lives and multiple addictions in an effort to rekindle community.[1]

Over the years we've had to take on board that it's not just some of our trainees who wrestle with alcohol. The organisation has also had to develop its policy, and we've changed our culture so that drink is no longer normalised at social functions.

What we have learned is that alcohol addiction isn't something that individuals should have to deal with in isolation. It's a social issue for which we need to shoulder collective responsibility.

In GalGael we haven't found that easy. A dry Burns Supper like the one we held the other night isn't Scotland's most intuitive claim to fame. But what many people remarked on was how they didn't feel the lack of a dram. It was really quite something, as poetry and song started to pour out from folk who might otherwise have had to exclude themselves.

I'm not a teetotaller, but I do think we need more events that are safe social spaces for everyone – and not just for recovering alcoholics, but also for those who avoid drink for cultural or personal reasons.

In GalGael we've found you don't need to be the proverbial 'drunk man' looking at the thistle to see Scotland's soul.[2] But you do need that deeper solidarity with fellow humankind that Rabbie Burns was all about.

Notes:

1. GalGael Trust: www.galgael.org

2. 'A drunk man looks at the thistle', Hugh MacDiarmid

Haiti and *The Road*

According to the website apocalypticmovies.com, 2010 is a bumper year for end-of-the-world films, with nine being released, starting with *The Road*, in January.[1]

The Road is about a father and son fleeing from some unspecified disaster. For me it was disturbing, not out of fear of apocalypse, but for how it portrays humanity – as the father elevates his gun to a fetish-like status with a dog-eat-dog stance towards others on the road.

Is this really what people are like? Or is it more a film-maker's projection of individualistic North American gun culture?

One answer came just four days after the movie's release as the Haiti earthquake struck. Camera teams rushed in, many expecting footage of barbarous infighting.

But that initial media angle is now being criticised. The reality, as the Disasters Emergency Committee told me yesterday, is that *'The vast majority of Haitians responded with enormous dignity and patience, not fighting for food but helping one another.'*

What's more, Obama swung into action with ten thousand American military mobilised, and here in the UK we've so far voluntarily given sixty-seven million – more than a pound for every person in the country.

The word 'apocalypse' is a theological word, with a double meaning. It means catastrophe, for sure, but also, revelation. Only when put to the test is it revealed who we are as human beings.

Right now, the vast majority of Haitians are revealing to the world just what they're made of.

Who knows what would be revealed if a similar catastrophe were to strike Scotland, but there's one thing of which we can be sure. Every time we act decently towards one another we strengthen resilience in our communities and with it, our capacity to cope with whatever happens.

That kind of survival skill counts for more than any gun, and we don't have to wait for calamity before it pays dividends.

Note:

1. Based on the novel *The Road*, by Cormac McCarthy

Feed my people

By this time tomorrow it'll all be over and the electoral dust will start to settle. One thing is sure. In the wake of the credit crunch the winner is going to have to take some very tough decisions. Political courage will be needed, but values too.

I wonder: what might inspire those values?

It's a question that hit me forcibly last week. You see, I'm a Commissioner on Scotland's Poverty Truth Commission. The Commission brings people who struggle in life face-to-face with those who have some power to make a difference, and it has support from all of Scotland's main political parties.[1]

One of the Commission's subgroups examines the links between ingrained poverty and violence. We'd been invited to meet with some community leaders in the Cranhill and Ruchazie area of east Glasgow.

They told us how little there is for the youth to do there, and how much they'd love to have a football pitch.

After the meeting I left with my friend Paul Chapman, who's a clergyman from New York. Sitting outside on the steps were four girls waiting for their youth club to begin. We paused to say hello. They asked where we were from and immediately pressed Paul with questions about New York's bright lights and celebrity culture.

They were just twelve to fourteen years old, dressed like any other teenagers ... but something bothered me. Three of the four of them had profoundly furrowed brows.

It looked like all the burdens of a weary lifetime had prematurely etched their mark. I came away angered, and thinking, 'So, *this* is the human face of poverty in Scotland!'

I just hope that whoever gets in tomorrow pauses a moment and centres their values, before deciding on whom they will have to turn the heat. Jesus simply said, 'Feed my people,'[2] and so ... recall those four wee Scottish lassies, and read what is written on the foreheads of our most hard-pressed youth today.

Notes:

1. The Poverty Truth Commission: www.povertytruthcommission.org

2. John 21:15–19

Outside the box

On Monday night my wife and I had a friend who's a Buddhist monk round for dinner. Not so long ago we'd have had outlandish conversations where I'd be looking for some crazy way to subvert his teachings, and we'd all tumble into laughter.

But in recent years he's developed Parkinson's disease. His hands now shake uncontrollably and his voice has become so soft that, together with my need to wear hearing aids, we must have looked a right pair struggling to have a conversation.

His condition's been stabilising, but he said that during the worst times he'd felt like both his body and mind were being progressively closed up inside a box.

Such medical conditions force the question: are we just physical entities – egos on legs – here today, gone tomorrow? Or is there more to life than that? Do we also have a soul that's outside of any box? And my friend and I just laughed about this because such a realisation, so often stirred by adversity, is precisely what the spiritual journey's all about.

Then, yesterday morning I caught the edge of a radio debate about party political compromise. A politician was clinging to what she called 'the spirit of the manifesto' – the box of her own party's set ideas. But the interviewer was pressing her on what he called 'the spirit of fairness' – the need also to do politics from outside of the boxes in which we might have become trapped.

And I thought about my friend with Parkinson's: and how one way or another we're all boxed in, whatever our station in life – and that the only way out is to seek a deeper way through … and perhaps that's a lesson for us all from my friend the Buddhist monk.

Eating and drinking

Here in Glasgow it's the start of the school holidays, and all across the land the festive spirit of summer is breaking out.

I myself will be heading down to Wiston Lodge near Biggar this weekend for something called the Solas Festival.[1]

It's a new idea for round here – a weaving together of the arts, a passion for justice … and faith.

Music from such bands as the Peatbog Faeries will vie with talks from radical Christians, serving politicians, a prominent Muslim leader and a Jewish climate change activist currently standing trial for blocking the runway at Aberdeen airport. And there'll be – dancing!

Too often in Scotland's past there's been this grim idea that dancing and religion don't mix. You've heard it before: we fear dancing lest it leads to sex … and sex lest it leads to dancing!

Yet Jesus himself had no time for such upright uptightness. In the Gospels of both Matthew and Luke he challenges the emotionally cold and religious, quoting to them: 'We played the flute for you, and you did not dance; we sang a dirge, and you did not cry.'[2]

And he tells how John the Baptist fasted and was teetotal, yet they did him down. But when Jesus himself came 'eating and drinking' they were just as small-minded, saying, 'Here comes a glutton and a drunkard, a friend of tax collectors and sinners.'[3]

Well, I don't think there'll be too much gluttony and drunkenness at Wiston Lodge this weekend. But there may be tears at some of the talks about the state of the world, and if I get on my feet to the music, there'll certainly be amusement: as an old girlfriend once told me, 'You dance like a spider in labour.'

Oh, what a long way some of us Scots have yet to go! May our summer festivals loosen us up. Grant us more such spiritual abundance.

Notes:

1. Solas Festival: www.solasfestival.co.uk

2. Matthew 11:17, Luke 7:32

3. Matthew 11:19, Luke 7:34

Woe to them

As the G8 summit closed in Canada this past week, Oxfam issued a statement saying, *'No maple leaf is big enough to hide the shame'* of the rich world's failure seriously to tackle world poverty.

For me it brought back memories of the G8 summit in Scotland five years ago. Nearly a quarter of a million of us filled the streets of Edinburgh demanding action on climate change and a fair deal for Africa.[1]

Thousands then headed off to Gleneagles, as George Bush and Tony Blair helicoptered in. I took winding back roads, passing near-derelict farmsteads where I know from locals that an absentee landlord had forced his tenant farmers out.

It made me think that poverty happens when people lose their asset base. What sends Africa to the G8 isn't a million miles removed from Scotland too.

This came back to me last Thursday when the *New York Times* ran an article reporting that 71% of those buying landed estates come from outside of Scotland.

But what rankles most is its description of Scottish property as *'a trophy, for the bankers with their big bonuses ... back on track after 18 quiet months'*. And it recommends buyers that if you *'visit only a few weeks a year'* you can always *'hire a couple of local people'* to *'generate enough cash to cover costs and to look after the wildlife'*.[2]

There you see it. The land that should support whole communities boils down to a housekeeper and a gamekeeper.

To me that's more than just an economic issue. It's also spiritual. As the prophet Micah said: *'Woe to them that ... covet fields ... and houses, and take them away: so they oppress ... even a man and his heritage.'*[3]

The dispossessed need justice, not handouts from the G8. All I can say is thanks to the *New York Times* for showing us why Scotland's land reform legislation needs to be kept – on track.

Notes:

1. 'Thousands flock to poverty march', BBC News, 2 July, 2005 http://news.bbc.co.uk/1/hi/uk/4642053.stm

2. 'Scotland offers deluxe haven to the rest of Britain', by Richard Holledge, June 24, 2010, *New York Times* http://www.nytimes.com/2010/06/25/greathomesand destinations/25iht-rescot.html?pagewanted=all&_r=0

3. Micah 2:1–3

Femininity of God

There's been a flurry of media excitement as an archaeological dig on Westray in Orkney has yielded up a second five-thousand-year-old 'Venus' figure – like one found last year, locally nicknamed 'the Wife of Westray'.[1]

Peter Yeoman of Historic Scotland was quoted as saying that these *'well-endowed ladies'*, as he delicately put it, are *'generally recognised as images of deities'* that might *'start to allow us to consider the spiritual life'* of our distant ancestors.

Marija Gimbutas, a controversial Lithuanian-American professor of archaeology, held that in prehistoric Europe the deity was a feminine, egalitarian and peace-loving life force … until groups of men sold on violence domesticated the horse to extend the reach of war, and, at the same time, recast God in their own violently patriarchal image.[2]

Most archaeologists consider that Gimbutas overplayed the feminist hand. Yet I have to say that, as a man concerned with gender justice, something inside me closes down whenever I hear God referred to exclusively as male.

What I find inspiring is the biblical tradition that we're made in 'the image of God', both male and female:[3] that the Holy Spirit in Hebrew and Greek is gendered feminine;[4] that chapter 38 of Job twice pictures the *womb* of God as bringing forth the wonders of creation;[5] and that Jesus identified himself with woman wisdom,[6] and with the tender image of a mother hen sheltering chicks under her wing.[7]

We may never know what the Orkney Venuses really mean, but something ancient and untameable stirs in me to hear they've surfaced ... a reminder, perhaps, that God is not just male, but female too ... for God is the essence of what gives life.

Notes:

1. www.historic-scotland.gov.uk/orkneyvenus

2. Gimbutas, *The Civilization of the Goddess and Other Works.* I explore the abuses and uses of Gimbutas on pp.119-121 and 130 of my book *Hell and High Water: Climate Change, Hope and the Human Condition*, Birlinn, 2008

3. Genesis 1:27

4. Hokmah (Hebrew), Sophia (Greek) – gendered feminine and translated as 'wisdom' or sometimes 'woman wisdom', as when personified, e.g. in Proverbs 8

5. Job 38:8, 29

6. Matthew 11:19; Luke 7:35

7. Luke 13:34

Right speech

Anybody with a heartfelt affection for British-Pakistani relation-ships will be saddened by the ongoing fracas in the world of cricket.

On Sunday the chair of the Pakistan Cricket Board controver-sially said that some English players have taken money to lose a game and influence the betting. His remarks embarrassed many in Pakistan as much as they angered the English. He based them on what he called *'loud and clear talk in bookie circles'*.[1] An already fraught situation thus became further poisoned by trading in gossip.

It's a funny word, 'gossip'. It comes from the Old English *godsibb*, meaning a 'godparent'. Originally, a gossip was supposed to have your spiritual interests at heart. Only in the sixteenth century did the meaning of the word change to denoting something malicious.

In the simple sense of talking about one another we all need gossip. It lubricates our relationships in community. But how can we test that our words are for shedding light, and not just heat?

The Buddhists teach a three-fold test of what they call 'right speech'. Ask yourself:

Is it necessary?

Is it true?

And, is it kind?

For me, to ask whether what I'm about to say is *necessary*, brings into focus the values I serve and what I desire to achieve.

To ask if it's true, pushes me to check the balance of my facts.

And to ask if it's kind ... I find that one's the hardest of all ...

because sometimes a necessary truth is a truth that hurts.

Perhaps what matters is not to confuse kindness towards somebody with simply massaging the surface of their ego. What matters is to do what you maybe have to do with a person, but to keep your heart open to them.

My goodness! Such demanding tests of right speech would drive the most of us to silence! But when you think about these tensions with Pakistan, any lesser standard just isn't cricket.

Note:

1. http://www.theguardian.com/sport/2010/sep/19/pakistan-chairman-england-one-day

Unique and precious

The spending cuts mean a grim future for many people over the next few years. My thoughts are with the vulnerable, and, as it happens, later on this morning I'm delivering a guest lecture to three hundred students at the Glasgow School of Art.

I'm wondering: what will the cuts mean for this generation of young artists?

It's been a hard week to defend their patch. At the Tate Modern in London a Chinese sculptor, Ai Weiwei, tipped a hundred million individually hand-painted porcelain sunflower seeds onto the floor so spectators could have the experience ... of walking all over them!

But the dust from their crushing went up the noses of Health and Safety, so now the whole exhibit's been cordoned off.

At first I thought, 'There goes another wacko modern art project!' But then I learned that Ai Weiwei had grown up in a forced labour camp. His poet father and his mother had been sent there by the Mao regime.

The young man saw that Chairman Mao had become a human idol. He'd become a blazing Sun to which the people constantly had to turn, as if they were his sunflowers.

Their individuality was crushed, and yet, like those hundred million seemingly identical, hand-painted sunflower seeds, each one of them was unique.

Today, much of the stuff we buy is 'Made in China'. Yet who are the individuals in the factories? Do we give a damn? Or do we just trample on, kicking up the dust, like in the Tate Modern where God-knows-who painted each sunflower seed.

But maybe that's the artist's point: God knows … who painted each sunflower seed.

It's said that when the ones in the Tate were walked over they made a crunching sound. I'm thinking of the numbers crunched in this spending review.

Every human being is unique – precious – no matter how invisible. God knows it. Let art show it. And the powerful not forget.

Community with a bang

It's a cruel irony that the kind of people who are going to feel the budget cuts announced this week are mostly not the sort who played the casino economy. In a more just world, those who made the killing would be paying back the nation's loss, but that's not the world we're living in.

The world we live in is where 'more work for less pay' will fall on people like council workers and civil servants – so called because they serve civil society, helping to keep the lives of us all … civilised.

Scotland today faces a time that will challenge the dignity and self-esteem of many, and I wonder … will those who get off lightly just pull up the drawbridge, or could we see a less selfish spirit emerging in the nation?

Recently I got an e-mail from my friend Maria, in West Papua on the other side of the world. She might be coming here to Govan to spend some time with local groups to learn about community regeneration.

But perhaps we'll be doing the learning too, because here's a story she tells about her village:

One day when she was seven her father was filtering petrol for their fishing boat, but forgot to extinguish his cigarette. The fag end dropped in the fuel tank, there was an almighty bang, their house went up in ashes … and it was on Christmas Eve!

But the village sprang into action. Men chopped down trees and women wove the fronds of sago palm into wall panels. Within twenty-four hours the house was restored, and it didn't cost her parents a penny.

Maria ends her e-mail saying, '*I believe that God is love, and that social capital exists, and that even if it has died we can still bring it back to life.'*

That's the kind of Christmas that's immune to budget cuts ... but it's up to us to call it back to life.

Phone hacking

To manage the news in the mass media is a huge responsibility. It means holding collective consciousness, indeed the social fabric of the nation, in one's hands.

I therefore find it astonishing that Gordon Brown reportedly still awaits a reply from the London Met as to whether or not one of Rupert Murdoch's newspapers hacked into his phone messages.

This past week has also seen the resignation from No.10's staff of Andy Coulson, who was Murdoch's former editor at *The News of the World*.

The Murdoch stable has a long history of political association. Prior to the 1997 general election it ran a headline: 'The Sun Backs Blair', and before long this was followed by nearly a whole front page in *The Sun* pressing a grateful Blair to 'Bomb, Bomb, Bomb' in Kosovo.

Well, it's a free country. But if it's the case that media power has hacked a prime minister's phone – potentially allowing democratic process to be second-guessed and influenced – then somebody's edging very close to the dictionary definition of treason.

There's another side of this that also bugs me: the ease with which a person's most intimate space can now be ripped open and tipped out onto the pavement for all to read the entrails.

Consider the police video of Gail Sheridan's interrogation that found its way here to the BBC. Whatever happened to her right to privacy?

The Roman Catholic mystic Thomas Merton had something to say about privacy.

Love, he said, means treating our neighbour *'with all the immense humility and discretion and reserve and reverence without which no one can presume to enter into the sanctuary of another's subjectivity'*[1] ... in other words ... into the intimacy of another person's private world.

That's the deeper issue behind the crime of phone hacking. Do we want to be a society that respects legitimate sanctuaries of one another's subjectivity, or do we condone their rape?

Perhaps Gordon Brown will shortly find out from the Met.

Note:

1. Thomas Merton, *Wisdom of the Desert*, W.W. Norton, NY, 1970, p.18

The smell of a field

Two key events for farming are happening today. In Edinburgh, the Church of Scotland is holding a conference to support Scottish farmers who want to produce food in sustainable ways, but see most of the public subsidies going to big agribusiness.

Meanwhile, in Manchester, the annual conference of the Soil Association has launched a new report called *The Lazy Man of Europe*.[1] It urges the UK government to end its neglect, and follow other European countries' encouragement of organic food and farming.

But why should the methods of food production matter? Is your breakfast egg not still an egg no matter how it's laid? Why pay extra for Kitemarks like Soil Association Organic, Fairtrade or the RSPCA Freedom Food label for animal welfare?

It's a question that reminds me of a fabled French-American joint space venture. There were the astronauts, zooming away in their rocket, the Americans sucking at toothpaste tubes full of nutrient paste, and the French, with their own on-board gourmet chef, and the Americans just couldn't understand why, for the French, food was more than just fuel.

The deeper meaning of food is about growing a world worth living in. To me, as significant as giving away money to charity is to affirm products mindful of the wellbeing of workers, communities, wildlife, farm animals and the soil. Charity only deals with the symptoms of injustice, but paying a fair price for right relationships tackles the root causes.

That's why, whether it's a field or a small allotment, sustainable food and farming matters to both the Soil Association and the Church of Scotland.

'See,' said the elderly Isaac in the book of Genesis: 'the smell of my son is as the smell of a field which the Lord hath blessed'[2]... and what better a blessing to ask upon a meal.

Notes:

1. www.soilassociation.org/conferences/2011conference/thelazymanofeurope

2. Genesis 27:27

The side God's on

This week saw the reopening of St Andrew's Cathedral in Glasgow, and what's captured imagination is painter Peter Howson's iconic likeness of St John Ogilvie, who in 1615 was brutally executed in Glasgow for his Catholic faith.

Howson's first attempt at the painting could easily have stirred up old sectarian tension. It showed a seething crowd of three hundred watching the martyrdom. But then, something came over the artist. He destroyed the crowd scene and focussed exclusively on Ogilvie.

The stunning result portrays a spiritual composure that both Catholics and Protestants have described as an invitation to prayer, a window into God. It's as if by taking the crowd out of the picture some great healing power forgave its historic complicity, and somehow releases us too from the violence of those times.

For sure, some might still ask: 'Whose side was God on?' but it's as if Howson's painting is reminding us that God is always on the side of those who suffer.

Now, fast forward, and this Saturday in Glasgow sees the launch of the report of the Poverty Truth Commission – a two-year project tackling deprivation in Scotland and stressing its roots in violence, child deprivation and social stereotyping.[1]

The title and the approach of the report is *'Nothing about us, without us, is for us'*, because poverty policy must work with people's resilience, courage and their community spirit.

The commissioners included Glasgow's Lord Provost, its Catholic Archbishop, the Moderator of the Church of Scotland, politicians, academics and some of the poorest people in the land.

For many commissioners it meant bridging a challenging social gap, but it worked – because of that same quality demonstrated in Howson's travail: namely, willingness to be on the side of those who suffer.

Note:

1. The Poverty Truth Commission: www.povertytruthcommission.org

Jesus and just war

Yet another, and another British soldier dies in Afghanistan. Meanwhile, in Libya, Colonel Gaddafi has confounded hope of being toppled, like Saddam's statue in Iraq, by a quick surgical jab.

On Sunday, William Hague conceded that there is *'no deadline'* to the Libyan mission, and that plans for a post-Gaddafi era are no further than the *'embryonic stage'*.[1]

And so these modern wars just rumble on, for most of us, like computer games running in the background.

Over the past fifteen years I've guest lectured, as a Quaker pacifist, on advanced military training courses across Europe. I've been surprised by the reception.

'Go tell the politicians,' some of the most senior officers will say, 'that war is a poor substitute for political policy to sort out other people's problems.'

They view themselves as peacemakers, so they'll ask: 'Can nonviolence bring anything *realistic* to the table?'

'It may not stop the immediate killing,' I'll say, 'but neither does war. Nonviolence operates at a deeper level. It seeks to take away the causes of war.'

It offers civil defence tactics, like Norwegian teachers used in resisting Nazi indoctrination. Nonviolence training prepares unarmed citizens to enter trouble spots, and gives local leaders the civic skills and *strength of soul* that can help restore justice, instead of throwing petrol on the fire, fighting evil with more evil.

It may sound bonkers, but that's what's bringing change in Egypt, and established black civil rights in America, and lowered the Iron Curtain, and ejected Marcos from the Philippines, and a growing list of other examples.

It was St Augustine who invented the 'just war' theory, saying: *'We go to war that we may have peace.'*[2] But Jesus never taught just war theory. Jesus taught nonviolence: for any fool can live in conflict – it takes guts to live in peace.

Notes:

1. http://www.theguardian.com/world/2011/jun/05/no-libya-military-deadline-william-hague

2. Augustine's A.D. 418 Letter 189:6 to Count Boniface, Roman Tribune of Africa: BBC translation: www.bbc.co.uk/ethics/war/just/history.shtml

For my military staff college addresses on nonviolence, see popular version here: http://www.alastairmcintosh.com/articles/2003--power-love.htm, and military ethics textbook version here: www.alastairmcintosh.com/articles/2010-McIntosh-Nonviolence-UK-Defence-Academy-web.pdf

The touch of blessing

Tomorrow is Father's Day – and thinking about it magnified my memory of a tiny event out in the garden. I'd gone to tip some clippings into the compost bin.

These days I live in a city, so I specially seek to stay in touch with nature.

Often I'll run my fingers through the compost, gently turning it over and enjoying, for a moment, the heaving mass of red-striped tiger worms, winding centipedes and countless other little critters whose world emerges from the coffee grounds and carrot tops, and all those other leftovers that would otherwise be stuffed as waste into a landfill site rather than giving life.

I went to put my tools away, but just as I was turning back indoors noticed that I'd hung the hoe up with its sharp end turned outwards.

Then it felt as if my father's hand was on my shoulder, or the hand of one of the old men back in my village on the Isle of Lewis.

A voice in my mind's ear whispered: 'Turn that hoe around, laddie, lest it cuts somebody.'

It wasn't a reprimand, and I'm hardly now a laddie. It was just the way a living culture hands things down and keeps a spark alive deep inside you.

More than just a hand of guidance, it was also the touch of blessing.

I thought: this is how it's meant to be, for it takes a whole community to father or mother a child.

Not all of us have someone to relate to on Father's Day. But we can all choose to make compost – that nourishing of what gives life that feeds community ...

There might we find our wider family.
To give and receive the touch of blessing.
Now, and down the generations.
Amen

You'll have had your tea

Today is the United Nations' World Refugee Day. The catchline is 'Real People, Real Needs' – because, of course, refugees are real individuals just like you and me.

I wonder, what does the term 'refugee' evoke in your mind? And what of 'the stranger'?

Here in Scotland, there's a famous city with a famous neighbourhood with a famous standing joke ... that an afternoon visitor is likely to be received with the response: 'You'll have had your tea.'

In other words, 'Don't come here expecting too much!'

It's not been true of that neighbourhood in my experience; but generally it very often is true that our first response to a stranger in need is: 'You'll have had your tea.'

But the power of facing honestly our own negativity is that it presses us to overcome such meanness of spirit.

For the way we treat a stranger shows us who we are. And if the reflection back troubles our peace, then let that be the gift that urges us to grow upwards.

In the tradition of the Celtic lands there are two sacred duties.

Hospitality for the short term, and fostership for permanence.

The infant Jesus was a refugee when his family fled to Egypt, escaping Herod's edict to destroy the little boys.[1]

And by adoption Joseph took him into David's line. Only then could prophesy be fulfilled.

There's a Gaelic proverb: *'Often, often,'* says the lark, *'goes Christ in the stranger's guise.'*

We may not all be Christians, but other religions based on love say much the same …

May we not miss the face of God, wherever real people have real needs, this World Refugee Day. Amen

Note:

1. Matthew 2:16

The Hebridean sun blessing

This dawn is summer solstice – and a very good morning to all who might be gathered at ancient sacred sites.

I grew up on the Isle of Lewis near the Calanais standing stones.

It beats most locals why visitors want to perform rituals there, often in rain and midges! But in keeping with the spirit, here's a story for celebrants at this morning's festivities:

Around 1695 the geographer Martin Martin spoke to a Lewis minister whose parish extended to the now-uninhabited Isle of North Rona.[1]

The minister on a visit had been greeted with: *'God save you, pilgrim, you are heartily welcome here; for we have had repeated apparitions of your person among us, and congratulate your arrival in this our remote country.'*

Then one of the men, who took their surnames from the *'colour of the sky, rainbow and clouds'*, processed around him, sunwise, uttering blessings of happiness. Then they gave him costly gifts of corn, *'as an expression of our sincere love'*.

While their intentions touched the minister, he was troubled by their Hebridean sun blessing and bade them to give it up.

But I wonder, might there not be a more integrated view? To early Christians, the sun often symbolised God.

Said Clement of Alexandria: *'Hail, oh light for he who rides over all creation is the "Sun of Righteousness" who has changed sunset into sunrise, and crucified death into life'*[2]

Let that be my summer solstice prayer.

And might our religion, whatever it may be, serve, in those rainbow words from North Rona, ... 'as an expression of our sincere love'.

Amen

Notes:

1. Martin Martin, *A Description of the Western Islands of Scotland circa 1695*, Birlinn Ltd, Edinburgh, 1994, pp.100–104

2. From *Saving Paradise: How Christianity Traded Love of This World for Crucifixion and Empire*, Rita Nakashima Brock & Rebecca Ann Parker, Beacon Press, Boston, 2008, p.173

The bonds of milk

Fifty years ago in Hamburg a pop group got together to record a song. It took a few years to be released, but reflected one of the iconic themes of the sixties cultural revolution.

It was called 'Nobody's Child', and the group which backed the singer (Tony Sheridan) would soon achieve fame as the Beatles.

I can still remember how at school a Scottish version of the same song drew tears from the girls.

It's about a youngster in an orphanage who is nobody's child: *just a lost flower growing wild, with no mother's kisses and no father's smiles, nobody wanting this nobody's child.*

To understand the sixties and what followed you've got to put them in the context of two world wars. Musicians like the Who with *Tommy* and Pink Floyd with *The Wall* could see that ridding the world of war must start with every child being loved.

The other day I was round at friends here in Glasgow. Something took me by surprise. The husband passed a plate and asked: 'Would you like a biscuit, made by my daughter?'

It was an utterance of such total normality ... yet the daughter is a teenage refugee – a 'nobody's child' fleeing traumatic violence in Africa.

A Gaelic proverb says the bonds of milk (of nurture) are stronger than the bonds of blood (of nature). Another says blood lineage counts for twentyfold, but fostership, a hundredfold.

Christ, you ask us who our neighbour is; and who, our true family.
Remind us of the proverb of the milk.
Help us make a world in which no child is a nobody's child.
Amen

Waiting for the New Age

Earlier this year the St Louis Sisters in Dublin invited me to hold a sharing with them about the spirituality of advanced old age.

I warned that I'm an impostor. I'm no expert in the matter. It's just I've found myself pushed in.

My Auntie Ann is ninety-two years old, and it was getting hard to find things to talk about with her. She's going deaf and blind; but one day, those very obstacles prompted me to suggest reading to her – from the Bible.

My goodness! As I did so, her face shifted into ecstasy! Even if she couldn't make out every word, her familiarity with the texts brought us together.

I asked about old age and dying. 'I'm not worried about old age,' she told me. 'I know where I'm going. I'm waiting for the *New Age*!'

Recently I've been talking to a lot of very old people, like the widows of the men I grew up amongst. Many are racked with loneliness, bereavement, loss of bearings and control, and distress at unfinished business.

Most yearn for spiritual deepening, but often there's a lack of pastoral support from those around, a stuckness when it comes to death and dying.

I said to the St Louis nuns, who'd spent their lives as school teachers: 'In the past you gave yourselves to the young. Maybe now it's time to work on the spirituality of old age.'

A time of life's completion.
Of preparation for birth into the New Age.
The pains of dying may give cause for fear.
But come to us in our vulnerability, God.
Teach us how to take away the fear of death.
Amen

The last head of standing corn

Yesterday I told of a sharing with St Louis Sisters in Dublin about pastoral care in the final stages of life. But we also talked of what the elderly can do for us.

The Gaelic word for old woman is *cailleach*. But it has a deeper meaning: 'holy old woman'; and also a more obscure meaning: 'the *cailleach*' was the last head of standing corn in the field – that which might be dry and wizened but would pass down the seedcorn.

So I said to these Irish sisters, these *cailleachs*, for their average age was about seventy: 'Tell me, what seedcorn has disposed fifty of you to give up half a day to share with a Protestant-raised Quaker who isn't even a nun?'

An electric ripple ran through the room as the first woman said: 'Recognition.'

'Recognition, of what?' I asked.

And they all clamoured in: 'Recognition that we still have something to offer.' 'Recognition that vocation doesn't end with retirement.' 'Recognition that nobody is ever so old that they cannot sit by another's bedside, or be present to the world in prayer.'

The Bible has stories that a woman came to Jesus with a jar of perfume.[1] She tenderly massaged his feet with tears and flowing hair. The Pharisees mocked, but Jesus pointed out a symmetry.

He said she was anointing him for his death, and that after her death, this simple loving act is what she'd be remembered for.

He also said: 'She has done what she could ... she has done something beautiful to me.' ...

May we never think ourselves so old that we cannot offer what little we can.

May we learn the arts of doing beauty – to each other.

May age reflect the ripening of our love.

Amen

Note:

1. Luke 7, Mark 14, Matthew 26, John 12

A pregnant social significance

Scotland's higher education is in the news, with students protesting cuts in the humanities at Glasgow and Strathclyde universities, and the First Minister citing Burns: that *'the rocks will melt with the sun'* before he'll bring in tuition fees for Scots.

So ... we hear what is wanted. We want to be an educated nation because we disdain ignorance. We want a subject range that includes science and business, but also offers the social sciences and the humanities. And we want our children to have it without being loaded up with mortgage-sized debts.

But wait a minute ... has the world not changed? Is everybody not just out for themselves now? If education buys power and influence, ought it not be paid for at the market rate, and specialise in subjects that serve ... that same market?

That's the managerialist view, but it's not a vision that offers life, or distinguishes a nation.

A Scots education is a precious thing. It needs to be understood and reclaimed. The Scots democratic intellect is a principle that the educated should serve the community and not become a self-serving elite. The Scots generalist tradition is that specialisms need the context of broad subjects like geography, history and philosophy – so that the young can better get their bearings in the world that they are called to navigate.

It is one thing to learn how to build a missile system and be taught skills of competition in the arms trade. But quite another to have an education system that confers the wisdom to discern what we should be doing in the first place.

When Mahatma Gandhi was asked what filled him with the greatest despair, he said: *'The hard-heartedness of the educated.'*

So, what is the way forward? I know where I stand. I'm with John Blackie, a professor of Greek, who told Edinburgh's town council in 1855: '*We demand a scholarship with a large human soul and a pregnant social significance.*'

Decolonising the soul

It would seem that the youth in English cities this week have been rioting not for bread, or for social justice, but for consumer goods that sell an identity; and burning down their own neighbourhoods in the process.

So, what is going on? Bear with me while I share a weird story.[1]

One day in his travels Jesus met a madman who could not be bound by chains, who cried out amongst the tombs of the dead and cut himself with stones.

In other words, like many young people tortured by broken lives today, he was self-harming.

His name was Legion, and Jesus cast out his Roman legion's worth of devils and turned them into a herd of pigs, which then ran down a hill and drowned.

I said it was a weird story … and what's weirder is that the Jews didn't eat pigs, so who did? Most likely the Roman colonisers, who had decimated the male population where the madman lived.[2]

The 'demons' can be seen as inner manifestations of the violence that colonised this man's outer world. What started off as a medical story suddenly turns political.

Oppression that is inflicted by power from above is called 'vertical violence', but often, when it cannot be tackled vertically, the consequences lash out sideways as 'lateral violence': violence against one's own community, family and even self.

Could it be that this week's lateral violence cannot be separated from the powerful of the land having set up false gods of 'greed is good', and that these have been tumbling down in a succession of national scandals?

If so, our task is to decolonise the soul, to restore truth and integrity and to offer every child a future that builds social cohesion.

But that is not an easy task. For if we cease to worship, or 'show worth' to our idols, we are left with a challenging question: to what kind of a 'god' might we 'show worth' instead?

For what do our values stand?

Notes:

1. Mark 5:1–20

2. During the Jewish Revolt of 66 AD, Josephus in *The War of the Jews* (Bk 7): *'So Vespasian marched to the city of Gadara. He came into it and slew all the youth, the Romans having no mercy on any age whatsoever. He set fire to the city and all the villas around it.'* Although the massacre took place after the death of Jesus, it probably happened shortly prior to the writer of Mark putting pen to paper. As such, the Gospel's author may have engaged in contextual theology: setting an older story into a context that refreshed its meaning for his readers.

To touch the hearts of all

Although I was only eight when President Kennedy was assassinated, I can remember where I was because I was in hospital. A 'Nurse Kennedy' told me, and with it being Stornoway, I thought they must be related, which was why it cut a notch in my memory.

This Sunday marks the tenth anniversary of 9/11, and as with President Kennedy, many of us can probably remember where we were at the time.

Within a month the US had invaded Afghanistan, but is the world a safer place ten years down the line? Certainly not for thousands of Afghan civilians who have lost their loved ones in this conflict, or for the families of soldiers who will never return home.

But if we're not going to throw petrol on the fire, what can we do when struck by violence?

Many years ago I was working in a country racked by poverty and social breakdown. I used to attend the small Quaker meeting there. One night one of our members, a seventeen-year-old Australian girl, found herself surrounded by a gang of fourteen youths.

She was sexually assaulted and left lying on a hillside.

The police would normally have gone in and brutalised their squatter settlement. But she asked them not to retaliate. Instead, she wanted something that might ... 'touch their hearts'.

Her father asked me to go with him to their camp. We went in unarmed, and asked them how best we could all seek reconciliation.

On the appointed day the fourteen young men headed a procession down to where we lived, with their entire community walking behind them, amidst much beating of drums.

One by one they filed past us. Many were in tears, and each in his own language said, 'I'm truly sorry.'

You couldn't help but feel that few would re-offend, and that the girl had reclaimed something precious in her life.

As for 9/11 ... can we not go deeper than a bullet to the heart ... and seek instead to touch the hearts of all?

Honesty as honesty's price

As the credit crunch bites in Greece, the media's filled with reports of boarded-up building sites, closed down shops, heaped up rubbish and even hunger touching the most vulnerable people.

One part of me thinks how tax evasion is said to be 'a Greek national sport', and that's a large part of why their government may run out of money by November.

But another part of me says to cut the *schadenfreude*. As recently as 1974, Greece was a military dictatorship. Freedom there is still in its youth, and who knows what fires might be set loose within Europe were it to be lost again.

In any case, where would you or I stand if we too could dodge our taxes so easily?

This is October, the month of the Inland Revenue's deadline if you submit your tax return on paper. I'm self-employed. I've just done mine, and you know, every year I find it a moral challenge!

I sit in my office surrounded by piles of receipts. 'I can put that one through as a business expense,' says a voice in my mind.

'No, you shouldn't,' says a second voice, so I chuck it in the bin.

'But you're cheating yourself!' protests the first voice, and I pull the receipt back out again to put it through the books.

'Are you really sure that's honest?' asks the second voice ... because honesty is what it comes down to, quite apart from the penalties of being found out.

Recently when I was back home on Lewis an old woman gave me a book of spiritual reflections by C.H. Spurgeon.

'Success through questionable transactions must always be hollow and treacherous,' Spurgeon says, for *'if we lose inward peace, we lose more than a fortune can buy'*.[1]

Honesty is the cost of honesty. If we let it slide, if we trade our honesty for gain against the common good, it is social stability that goes. The lessons of Greece show how much can hinge on inner peace.

Note:

1. C.H. Spurgeon, *The Cheque Book of the Bank of Faith*, Christian Focus Publications, Tain, 1996, p.336 (Rather more fundamentalist than my usual reading, but given to me in a beautiful spirit.)

Animal spirits

According to a recent survey from Scottish Natural Heritage, the animal that people link most strongly with Scotland is the deer.[1]

But more than half of us are not comfortable with them being hunted.

Well, growing up on the Isle of Lewis I used to be a stalker's ghillie, bringing the carcases down off the hill with a pony.

Now. at fifty-six, I'm living in Glasgow, but a couple months ago I succumbed to an urge to go back to my old job. Tommy Macrae, the keeper who once trained me, has since gone to the Happy Hunting Grounds, but his widow invited me to stay, and I spent a week with her son, Christopher, who's now taken over.

I confess to huffing and puffing up the hills, but what I saw left me persuaded that deer hunting as we have it today is part of animal welfare.

The point is that stags don't wear condoms! If the herds aren't culled for meat, they slowly starve in winter, and it's a sorry sight to watch them stumble on incredibly skinny legs along the shore, scraping for seaweed to survive.

The week I went back to my old job I worked with four stalkers. These men had an incredible respect and even reverence for the land. Back at the larder after the day's work we'd raise a glass, and the toast would be: 'To the Soul of the Stag'.

She's a godly woman is old Tommy's widow who looked after me, and that makes me think of how Isaac said to Esau in the book of Genesis: *'Bring me venison ... that I may eat, and bless thee before the Lord before my death.'*[2]

There you see the cycle of life, blessing and death. We and the deer are interdependent, bound up in the balance of nature.

That's why I'm pleased to hear that a new study reveals the deer to be our most iconic animal.

I raise my glass: 'To the stalkers of Scotland ... to animal welfare ... to the Soul of the Stag'.

Notes:

1. 'Deer most recognised Scottish animal, survey finds', BBC News, 23 November, 2011, www.bbc.co.uk/news/uk-scotland-highlands-islands-15852644

2. Genesis 27:7, KJV

The utility of wealth distribution

A report out this week says that Britain should tax the rich to tackle the income gap between the rich and poor.[1]

It might be easy to dismiss it as yet another leftie response to the economic crisis, but this time it's from the OECD, the Organisation for Economic Co-operation and Development, which is committed to market economics and grew out of the Marshall Plan that rebuilt Europe after the Second World War.

The report says that since 1975 inequality has risen faster in the UK than in any other high-income country. The top ten percent of us average fifty-five thousand pounds a year compared with the bottom ten percent on less than five thousand.

Now, many years ago I did an MBA at Edinburgh University. The economics lecturer taught us about *'the diminishing marginal utility of wealth'*! The theory goes that the more dosh you've already got, the less utility each marginal or extra dollop has, and that's why the rich need to earn more and more.

What got me was that the economists never thought of turning it around and considering 'the increasing marginal utility of wealth redistribution'!

Last week we celebrated St Andrew's Day, and one of the things Scotland's patron saint did was to introduce Jesus to the lad with the loaves and fishes.

By redistributing his surplus the lad increased its total utility. If others followed suit such wealth optimisation would indeed constitute the miracle that fed the five thousand.

It's cold today, and I live close to the BBC studios here in Govan where it's a fact that some neighbours – those near the bottom ten percent of income – can't afford to have their heating on.

What would happen if our politicians took heed of this week's OECD report? What if five grand were top-sliced from the rich and shared with the poor?

Might that not be an economic miracle that could feed the five thousand of today?

Note:

1. *Divided We Stand: Why Inequality Keeps Rising*, OECD, 2011: www.oecd.org/els/soc/dividedwestandwhyinequalitykeepsrising.htm

The spirituality of stillbirth

We so often hear the bad news, but I was heartened to learn yesterday that the rate of stillbirth in Scotland has fallen to less than five deaths per thousand deliveries.[1]

New Year's Day has never been the same for my wife and me these past five years.

Vérène was thirty-two weeks pregnant. We had gone to bed early on Hogmanay, but the next morning, her womb was motionless.

The radiologist at the Southern General turned on the scan. There was the outline of our little son, but no heartbeat.

I just said it … 'He's flown the nest, my dear.'

The staff were incredible. But what so shook me was how, during the delivery, I was swept up by a sacred sense of knowing this child intimately: some glimpse of life running deeper than death.

Today is Saint Bride's Day, the festival of Bridget or Bhrighde. Her many workers and charges include midwives and babies and children in difficulties, because, according to the Scottish version, this lass was flown by angels to the Holy Land to become the foster mother of Christ.

It's one of those crazy traditions, but I've learned that some of these stories can reveal spiritual depths unfathomable … like when you have to gaze beyond the life of your own child.

Alexander Carmichael, who collected Bridget tales from the Hebrides, saw this Celtic goddess and Christian saint as the time-less principle of life, death and rebirth.

He wrote that on her feast day each year, the first of February: *'Brigit with her white wand is said to breathe life into the mouth of the dead winter and to bring him to open his eyes to the tears and the smiles, the sighs and the laughter of spring.'*[2]

Today we welcome news from the NHS that stillbirth in Scotland has fallen to its lowest rate ever … But to families on the tragic side of the statistic, I'd urge: stay alive to those *'sighs and the laughter of spring'*.

Notes:

1. 'Scottish stillbirth rate lowest on record', BBC News, 31 January, 2012: www.bbc.co.uk/news/uk-scotland-16812200

2. *Carmina Gadelica*, Volume 1, by Alexander Carmichael, 1900

Midwives of transition

During the past few months there's been a string of scandals in the English press about how elderly people are treated in care homes and by the NHS. It's not been such an issue in the Scottish media, but I bet we'd be kidding ourselves if we think that everything is rosy this side of the border.

On Wednesday a pressure group, the National Pensioners Convention, published its Dignity Code.

Supporters include the heads of the TUC and the Royal College of Nursing, who have collectively written to the press saying: *'Many older people have seen their basic human dignity undermined – they have been treated as objects rather than people.'*[1]

They express concern not just about overt abuse, but about commonplace degradation of dignity like lack of hygiene and loss of privacy.

But what has become of us if we treat our fellow humankind as objects rather than people?

Is it just that we lack the resources to cope with an ageing society? Or is it much bigger than that? Does it hinge on what we think a human being is?

For if we see death as no more than a fizzling out of energy, can we really be surprised if people get treated as spent batteries? But what if people are more than just spent batteries? What if dying is the process of plugging in and switching over … to the spiritual mains?

A time, like birth itself, of great spiritual transformation?

Some people think that might be so. For example, an Edinburgh-based charity called Faith in Older People.[2]

If their faith-based view of later life is right, then those who do the caring are midwives of transition. They tread on holy ground. And who knows, that holy ground might be the gift of life's last days … to us all.

Notes:

1. 'Dignity code for OAPs', *The Telegraph*, 22 February 2012
http://www.telegraph.co.uk/health/elderhealth/9098176/Dignity-inspections-in-hundreds-of-care-homes-within-weeks.html

2. Faith in Older People: www.faithinolderpeople.org.uk

Archive of a nation's memories

I was in the middle of giving a lecture in Bratislava, the capital of Slovakia, the other day, when the news broke that Aung San Suu Kyi's party had swept the board in the Burmese elections.

I'd been asked to address the World Student Christian Federation. Youth from across Europe had come to reflect on where we're at in history, and how to heal the wounds of past totalitarianism.

On Friday we'd been shown round a cemetery by an old Slovakian Jew with eyes that shone with life, even as he told me of how he'd survived as a baby in Belsen, but had lost his mother there.

At the Nation's Memory Institute we were led by archivists through two kilometres of secret police files from the Nazi to the Soviet era that only ended with the Velvet Revolution of 1989.[1]

It felt eerie to flick through card indexes of folk whose lives had been put in chains, or worse, for standing up and standing out for freedom; eerier still to learn that in some European countries, their oppressors still hold public office.

In my lecture I'd used images of nonviolent resistance. One showed saffron-robed Burmese monks demonstrating five years ago with a banner that said: *'May all beings be free from danger and enmity. May they live peacefully.'* Halfway through I switched from Powerpoint to the BBC webpage, and we watched the news of the Burmese election breaking live.

The conference organiser was a Slovak woman who, like myself, is a graduate of Aberdeen University. I asked her what her thoughts were around their theme for next year.

'Maybe something about other faiths?' she suggested; and as I travelled back to Scotland, I thought of all those Buddhist monks, and these deep-thinking European youth determined that fascism should never rise again.

I thought: *These are the holders of the keys to peace*, and meeting them left me filled with hope.

Note:

1. Nation's Memory Institute: www.upn.gov.sk/english

The cuckoo of awareness

Have you heard the cuckoo yet? We're in the merry month of May, and this is meant to be the start of summer. So have you heard the cuckoo yet?

Last week scientists at the British Trust for Ornithology announced that they had tagged five cuckoos in order to map their migration route – their round trip was ten thousand miles, with a winter spent in countries like Congo and Cameroon.[1]

Over in Tibet, the cuckoo is a holy bird, the king of birds. The Buddhists even have a Temple of the Birds where grain is scattered, butter lamps are lit, and every spring the priests invite the cuckoo back to fill the mountains with its cry. An eighth-century sacred text called *The Cuckoo of Awareness* teaches that happiness is hidden somewhere deep within us all.[2]

And we in Scotland get a look in too. According to the Isle of Skye folklorist Otta Swire the cuckoo was a magical bird that spent its winters in the faerie hill, and its first port of call when summer came was the Callanish Stones.

When Otta was on Lewis in 1960 the cuckoo was late arriving. Everybody was asking: 'Have you heard the cuckoo yet? Have you heard the cuckoo?'

When it eventually appeared in mid-May there was a collective sigh of relief. It was as if, she says, 'all was well with the year': as if the right ordering of nature would now reflect in a right ordering of human affairs.

I mentioned this at a gathering here in Glasgow the other night. A man from the islands came up afterwards. He had a sorry family history – hard times, homelessness, prison and now a courageous daily fight against the bottle.

He said: 'I remember when we used to cut the peats. I'd always have an ear listening out for the cuckoo.'

'What did it mean to you?' I asked.

He answered with one word, a word that issued from his yearning for a life that's better ordered. It was wrenched from childhood memories, with emotions rippling like the wind across his face, and he said it with a relish that made me shake …

'Happiness!'

Notes:

1. 'Tagged cuckoos complete migration and return to the UK', Victoria Gill, BBC Nature News, 5 May, 2012: www.bbc.co.uk/nature/17895997

2. The Cuckoo of Awareness, by Vairocana, English translation by Karen Liljenberg: www.zangthal.co.uk/files/The_Cuckoo_of_Awareness.pdf

Faith and the land

There's been a flurry of activity around land reform these past few weeks with the community of Machrihanish taking over their own airbase, and North Uist exploring possibilities for the old Lochmaddy Hospital.

Next week the Isle of Eigg celebrates the fifteenth anniversary of its historic community buyout. I had some involvement with this, and recently was back on the island – this time with a delegation of provincial government planners who had travelled across the world from Indonesia.

Indonesia won its independence, after four hundred years of Dutch colonisation, in 1949, but through years of war. Decades of dictatorship followed, and only fairly recently has democracy gained a foothold.

The country's left with very top-down government, and that was why the delegation came to Scotland – to study governance from the bottom up.

It is no exaggeration to say that Eigg blew their minds. Since 1997 the population has increased by over fifty percent. The school and businesses flourish. Affordable housing means that the young are coming back to stay, and the island generates all its own electricity, mainly from renewables.

Indonesians are a very spiritual people and this group included followers of Islam, Christianity and indigenous religions.

We visited Eigg's newly restored Catholic church, used by residents of varying denominations. There Mairi, an island crofter, told how she'd spent eight years praying for the building to be saved.

It seems a very minor part of Eigg's history, yet the quality of her testimony touched the Indonesians to the core.

The provincial chief of planning got up, and said: 'If that woman had the faith to pray for eight years, then maybe there's hope for us too with the problems that we face.'

And so, congratulations to Eigg on its fifteenth anniversary of independence next week. Not everybody might be praying for you, but the rest will surely raise a glass.

The earth itself will teach you

Today's the longest day of the year – and a very happy summer solstice to all, including those who might be celebrating at Scotland's stone circles.

I've been reading tales about the Callanish Stones in Otta Swire's book of Hebridean legends.[1]

These days the family's best known through her son, Dr Jim Swire, who campaigns on the Lockerbie bombing that tragically took his daughter's life.

But Otta's own renown was in folklore. She tells of a time when her mother was staying at Stornoway Castle, and an antiquarian arrived to mount an expedition to the Callanish Stones.

He'd heard reports of strange goings on at Midsummer's Day, and that marriages first consummated at that time amongst the Stones were especially fruitful. But Lady Matheson, the wife of the island's then proprietor, Sir James Matheson, feared scandal, so she banned all her female guests from joining the excursion.

However, working at the castle was a maid said to be of one of the 'families of the Stones'. She told Otta's mother not to be disappointed, for 'only those to whom it is given may see'.

And sure enough, a thick fog descended, and all that the party of men experienced were eerie noises in the gloom, which proved to be a crofter's cow rubbing its backside on a rock!

Now, Callanish has a five-thousand-year-long spiritual history, and a few years ago, after duly communing with the Stones, I decided I'd pay a visit to the Callanish Free Church.

The young minister gave a mind-blowing sermon on Job 12 – that for sure, *'the wicked prosper in this world: but ask the animals and they shall tell you, or the earth itself and it will teach you ... that God ensures justice in the end.'*

My goodness, it left this Quaker quaking. To see all things connected. For as the bard MacDiarmid said: *'These bare stones bring me straight back to reality ... I lift a stone; it is the meaning of life I clasp.'*[2]

Notes:

1. Otta Swire, *The Outer Hebrides and Their Legends*, Oliver & Boyd, London, 1966, pp.24-26

2. Hugh MacDiarmid, 'On a Raised Beach', in *The Faber Book of Twentieth-Century Scottish Poetry*, ed. Douglas Dunn, Faber and Faber, London, 1992, pp. 56-68

The long blue wave

The Assyrian came down like the wolf on the fold,
And his cohorts were gleaming in purple and gold;
And the sheen of their spears was like stars on the sea,
When the blue wave rolls nightly on deep Galilee.[1]

These words from Byron gallop through my mind as the death toll in Syria approaches twenty thousand.

Yesterday the Arab League called on President Bashar al-Assad to stand down, but what else can be done?

Last month I was invited to the conference of the International Society for Military Ethics at the UK Defence Academy.[2] Many of the soldiers and academics could see a humanitarian case for military intervention in Syria, yet the impasses of Iraq and Afghanistan were hot on their minds. It is one thing for the former colonial powers to go in with all guns blazing. Quite another, to clear the political and psychological minefields left behind.

For me, Byron's poem leapt to life with that line about *'the blue wave'* that *'rolls nightly on deep Galilee'* – and how religion, so often an excuse for war, should properly be about taking away its causes.

Two years ago I met with a group of Syrian Orthodox priests in Beirut. 'What are you doing,' I asked them, 'to reduce the risks of future religious violence?'

'We meet regularly with our Muslim counterparts,' they told me. 'We have built up great respect for one another, and see such work as vital for the future of Syria.'

It left me thinking: war can be seductive on time's short wavelength, but it takes *the long blue wave* from such spiritual centres as 'deep Galilee', and from Mecca, to break the spiral of violence: to foster mutual respect, to build strong civic institutions in order that folk may eat from the Tree of Life, whose leaves, the prophets said, are *'for the healing of the nations'*.[3]

Notes:

1. Byron, 'The Destruction of Sennacherib'

2. Military on nonviolence: www.alastairmcintosh.com/articles/2010-McIntosh-Nonviolence-UK-Defence-Academy-web.pdf

3. Revelation 22:2 and Ezekiel 47:12

On Pussy Riot

Not content with having jailed the lead performers of Pussy Riot for disrupting a church service, the Russian police are reportedly now seeking other members of the band.

Punk rock does my head in, and when I first heard of these young women I took them as a tasteless publicity stunt.

But there was a niggle in my mind. In 2000 I was invited by the Russian Academy of Sciences and the Orthodox Church to lecture on the theology of Scottish land reform. At the cathedral where these women performed their act, I photographed a billboard. It was an image of a church with the caption: 'The Wall Street in Moscow'.

'What kind of an idolatrous icon is this?' I asked my hosts half jokingly, and they answered sadly that the oligarchs were busy buying up religious kudos.

In the past few days Pussy Riot's closing statements from the dock have gone on the Web. To me they're a stunning case of liberation theology – of theology that seeks to free that which gives life, by liberating theology itself.[1]

These young protestors challenge a domination system that does indeed try to buy religion to sanctify its crimes. In contrast, say the women, Jesus was a friend of prostitutes. He too was called crazy, got done for blasphemy, and turned the temple tables on the rich.

Pussy Riot speak from experience of politicians who destroy nature to build holiday homes, and of an education system that fails the wisdom of philosophy and the arts, and turns young people into automatons.

As one of the women told the court at her sentencing: *'I became fundamentally convinced of the priority of inner freedom as the foundation for taking action.'*

And another: *'People can sense the truth. Truth really does have some kind of ... superiority over lies and this is written in the Bible.'*

Amen! Lord, give us more such punk prayers.

Notes:

1. Closing statements: http://nplusonemag.com/pussy-riot-closing-statements

Celebrating Vatican II

I'm a Quaker, not a Roman Catholic, but tomorrow I shall celebrate the fiftieth anniversary of the start of a process within the Catholic Church called Vatican II.

This proclaimed that *'the joys and the hopes, the griefs and the anxieties'* of the poor and afflicted are shared by Christ, and *'the right of having a share of earthly goods sufficient for oneself and one's family belongs to everyone'.*[1]

Now, many of us might have agreed with George Osborne's speech this week where he looked towards a benefits system under which *'the shift-worker, leaving home in the dark hours of the early morning'*, would not have to look *'up at the closed blinds of their next-door neighbour sleeping off a life on benefits'*.[2]

But as he spoke, I was crossing the Minch on the Stornoway ferry with a close friend from school days. Desperate to find work, he was heading south for a job as a night watchman.

When we were boys he was the brightest, and the main difference in our situations today probably boils down to social class. I'd grown up as the doctor's son, with all its middle-class starts in life to help me 'get ahead'.

That's privilege for you, and that's the difference often overlooked in politics today.

In being drawn towards a world of greater justice I have been richly influenced by liberation theology. This grew from the seeds of Vatican II and it develops the principle that God expresses *'a preferential option for the poor'*. Before preaching, Jesus would ask if the people had been fed. He said *'inasmuch as you do it unto the least of these, you do it unto me'*. And in Luke 4 he proclaimed the year of Jubilee under which wealth was to be periodically redistributed.

As Roman Catholics celebrate the golden jubilee of Vatican II, may we, in these straitened economic times, resist the temptation to turn our backs on those who suffer. For these are those with whom the God of love resides in solidarity.

Notes:

1. *Gaudium et Spes (Joy and Hope),* Vatican II constitutional document promulgated in 1965 by Pope Paul VI, from paragraphs 1 and 69

2. www.channel4.com/news/osborne-unveils-10bn-benefits-cut-package

Learning how to love

The past ten days have seen thousands of people across England, Wales and Scotland forced from their homes by flooding. Last weekend I was visiting friends in the tiny Dumfriesshire village of Durisdeer. It was a Sunday morning, and we went together to the service at the parish Church of Scotland. The preacher was Michael Northcott, an Episcopalian down from Edinburgh University, and his sermon was on the flooding at Comrie in Perthshire.

As one of the Comrie community councillors told the press: '*Our Black Monday ... will go down as ... one of the bleakest seasons in the history of our community ... We have hundreds of residents deeply traumatised, fearful of the future and robbed of their homes.*'[1]

Perth Council is now working on flood defences to prevent a recurrence. But the crux of the minister's message at Durisdeer was the strength with which the Comrie folk were looking out for one another, because whole families are taking in other whole families until their homes dry out.

'Jesus didn't directly teach us to care for the earth,' was the culmination of the sermon that Sunday. 'Jesus taught us to love one another, and that's the only way we'll learn how to face the future by caring for the earth.'

I was left thinking back to three years ago to when the Comrie Development Trust ran a conference on climate change. They were looking at how to reduce the village's carbon emissions, but also at how to strengthen their community resilience – the ability to bounce back from any knocks, by pulling together.

That's the kind of preparation that's now paying off in Comrie. That's what makes this village at its time of greatest trial an inspiration to the whole of Scotland. And that too was the lesson from a tiny congregation in Dumfriesshire: the sheer imperative of learning how to love one another.

Note:

1. *Perthshire Advertiser*, 23 November 2012

Sir Patrick Moore, RIP

For many of us, for the greater part of our lives the astronomer Patrick Moore has been our messenger from the stars. He presented *The Sky at Night* continuously since 1957, and was one of the few people to have shaken hands with both the first man to fly an aeroplane, and the first man on the moon.

I vividly recall the excitement amongst us boys in Leurbost on the Isle of Lewis when the shopkeeper's son reported how on television he'd seen a fly come within the orbit of Patrick Moore's mouth; the mighty astronomer gave an almighty gulp, swallowed down the alien invader, and carried on the broadcast at Warp 7 without a blink. And I just loved finding the story confirmed in an obituary yesterday, along with his mother's wry conclusion: 'Yes, dear. It was nasty for you, but so much worse for the fly.'[1]

Patrick Moore was sceptical of claims that some astronauts had visions of God from their rockets. When asked what they might have been seeing, he said: 'I think they saw the moon.'

His evangelism was for outer space. But when I stand and look at the sky at night, my mind turns to inner space and to his famous dictum: *'We just don't know!'* For me, the wonder is that there's *something*, while cold logic would predict nothing.

To watch the shimmer of the Milky Way is to be reminded that our world, and all its worries, is held within the much vaster cosmological context that is the universe.

But if I turn the telescope around I sense, as well, the shimmer of a universe within, as if our lives are also held in some much greater consciousness.

Could that be the final beauty of the 'starry, starry night'; the love of which the poet spoke 'that moves the sun and all the other stars'?

Sir Patrick Moore is drifting back to stardust, but other worlds are where his Sky at Night leaves me.

Note:

1. 'Sir Patrick Moore', The Telegraph, 09 December, 2012

The Tree of Life

This week began with Epiphany – the revelation of Christ to the Gentiles as symbolised by the three wise men – and traditionally it's the time to take our Christmas trees down.

It's not just Christians who see trees and plants as a symbol of life. In the old Norse religion, Odin hanged himself from an ash tree for nine days to be granted the wisdom of the runes, and Rastafarians even maintain that the Tree of Life is – cannabis!

In the Hebrew Bible the Tree of Life grows from the heart of God's garden,[1] and Jesus called himself the Vine of Life, and we are its branches, in a symbol of profound spiritual interconnection.

How strange it is then, to walk the streets and see all these Christmas trees thrown out with the bins, blowing in the wind, as if the symbol of life itself has been discarded.

The imagery creates an air of desolation that strangely fits this time of year. January is a dark month for many. It can be a very lonely time, with people maybe dealing with the fallout of Christmas – family feuds, broken relationships, divorce, a suicide …

And yet, from underneath the ground the bulbs are breaking through. Already it's the snowdrops; and once when I was feeling down in winter, someone said to me: 'Think about the crocuses, Alastair.'

I look up at the trees too, and see their budding as a sign of new things coming; a reminder that there's more to life than just the cuts and blows that otherwise would hack a person down.

I noticed in the papers this week that the government is being urged to recognise the Scots pine as our national tree. Campaigners say that, like the Scottish people, it too *'comes in all shapes, colours and forms'*, and symbolises qualities to which we all aspire, like strength and wisdom.[2]

That's what the Tree of Life reminds me of, and why we decorate our homes in deepest winter. Life is not just birth and death, but resurrection too.

Notes:

1. Ezekiel 47, Revelation 22

2. Alan Watson Featherstone, quoted in *The Scotsman*, 9 January 2013

The imams of St Giles

The wave of bombings that left dozens dead in Baghdad yesterday reminds us that ten years on from the invasion of Iraq, life remains far from normal in that suffering country.

Recently I had cause to meet with Christian groups in Indonesia. There the Bible translates 'God' with the beautiful word Allah, but some of these Christians have every reason to fear the violent tensions that war has caused to ripple round the world.

What gives me heart this week, however, is news from Aberdeen. Would you believe it? The mosque beside St John's Episcopal Church is too small. Some of the Muslim faithful were having to pray outside. But St John's congregation said to their neighbours: 'Come on in and make use of our church!' – and that's what's been happening.[1]

Hallelujah!

But there's history behind this worth the telling. In 1991, at the end of the First Gulf War, the leaders of the mainstream Scottish Churches refused to ring their bells in jubilation. Instead they called a service of interfaith reconciliation at St Giles Cathedral. Scottish Muslims would have liked to come, but the timing of the service was going to clash with their evening call to prayer.

It was then that Dr Bashir Mann of Glasgow Central Mosque remembered a curious fact from Islamic tradition. When a delegation of Christians visited Medina in the year 631, they were allowed to pray in the mosque by the Prophet Mohammed (peace be upon him).[2]

The minister of St Giles was so impressed that he proposed to return the gesture, and it made news around the world when Scotland's Muslims held their call to prayer beside the Christian altar, as the rest of us gathered there for the service paid witness in prayerful silence. It was an amazing experience.

There you see the spirit that's come alive again today in Aberdeen. Let this speak louder to the world than all the brutal bombings! Allahu Akbar – 'God is Great' – 'and on earth, peace and good will to all'.[3]

Notes:

1. 'Christian church in Aberdeen is first in Scotland to share with Muslims', STV News: http://news.stv.tv/north/218052-aberdeen-christian-church-first-in-scotland-to-share-with-muslims/

2. See *The Fountain Magazine*, Issue 50/April–June 2005, 'Interactions between Prophet Muhammad and Christians', by Ismail Acar

3. Allahu Akbar is a central phrase of Islamic prayer. Usually translated 'God is Great' or 'Greatest', it is similar to 'Glory to God in the highest', which introduces my quote from Luke 2:14.

Blowing in the wind

As the Scottish Parliament today prepares to debate that *there is still such a thing as society*, and the dust of yesteryear lays to rest the life of Mrs Thatcher, I am struck this week by a different kind of dust that's been rising in the north-east.

On Tuesday, flights were disrupted at Inverness Airport, and roads around the Moray Firth had to be cleared by diggers because a combination of dry weather and high winds had caused the farmers' light and sandy soils to drift like snow.

I was speaking to an Aberdeenshire soil scientist yesterday, who thinks we rely too much on chemicals instead of natural fertility from crop rotation, composts and manure. We fail to build up humus in our soils, so they get too dry, and are blown away or washed far out to sea.

This lack of tenderness towards the land is nothing new. The old

Hebrew prophets railed against the practices that turned the Fertile Crescent into the deserts of the Middle East.

Isaiah said, '*The earth dries up and withers, the whole world withers and grows sick ... desecrated by the feet of those who live in it.*'[1]

And Jeremiah cried aloud: '*O land, land, land ... how long will the land mourn, and the grass of every field wither?*'[2]

It's not that farmers like to see their heritage a-blowing in the wind. The problem's deep in most of us. We want cheap food, we're used to cheap food, but aren't aware of what the cost could be to our children's future.

If I were speaking at today's debate in Holyrood, I'd be saying that society partly builds up from the soil, and asking: 'What support do farmers need to save the land from mourning?'

Yesterday, the Bishop of London quoted one of Mrs Thatcher's less well-known speeches, where she spoke of *interdependence* as the basis of society.

May that interdependence come on earth, as it is heaven, and right to the quality of the soil beneath our feet.

Notes:

1. Isaiah 24:4–5, NEB

2. Jeremiah 22:29; 12:4, NRSV

Saint Columba and the Cross today

Tradition holds that 1450 years ago this weekend, St Columba brought his Christian message from Donegal to Iona.

Amongst the celebrations marking this will be a conference of the Islands Book Trust on the Isle of Lewis exploring pilgrim links between Ireland and the Hebrides – and, this coming Sunday, a special thanksgiving service at Iona Abbey.

Afterwards, Historic Scotland will unveil the newly restored St Oran's Cross, now made whole again from fragments long-since broken.

When I stand beneath Iona's crosses, which have weathered nearly two-thirds of Christian history, they press me with a question: 'What might be the meaning of the Cross for us today?'

The answer lies in their ornate carvings – spirals hinting at the wellspring of Creation, interwoven knotwork revealing that all is one, and serpents that remind us that we only find a new life if we shed our outworn skins.

It was said to be the destiny of Saint Columba *'to lead the nations unto life'*.[1]

Today's Iona Community also celebrates a founding anniversary in 2013 – its seventy-fifth year of seeking *'new ways to touch the hearts of all'*. Like St Oran's Cross, restoring fragments of a world broken by poverty, violence and cruel discrimination on such grounds as race, sexual orientation or faith.

George MacLeod, who founded the Iona Community, had no doubt about the meaning of the Cross today. It stands, quite simply, for *'a power of love that's greater than the love of power'*.

That remains this holy island's message, 1450 years on from St

Columba's arrival. These high crosses – these stones that shout aloud from out their silence – call both nations and ourselves to life itself – to that *power of love that's greater than the love of power.*

Note:

1. Adomnán of Iona's *Life of St Columba*, Penguin Classics, 1995, III:3, p.207

Reality: real or virtual?

This is the first week in July, and when I was a boy on Lewis it used to be the most exciting time of the year – because it was the start of our summer holidays.

We'd be out in the boats with the old men hauling up the haddies with handlines, scrounging jammy pancakes and glasses of Creamola Foam from one another's mothers, and as we helped the neighbours gather in their peats we'd be hoping that Aitch wouldn't tell our dads if he caught us hitching a lift behind his tractor trailer on our bicycles.

Perhaps I was lucky, perhaps I have rose-tinted glasses, but I don't think I'm alone in remembering those days as a time when childhood meant innocence and trust, where doors were left unlocked and no one had to be told that it takes a whole community to raise a child.

But what about now? So many folks are working, so many are stressed and worried, that in the villages, and also on the city streets, it's difficult to build that important sense of community.

Children spend more time online, twittering with their Tweeter machines and with virtual reality standing in for the real thing.

There's even been a study in the news lately suggesting that the average age at which children first encounter pornographic content online is six, and there's the worry that the ease of availability normalises violence and exploitation in relationships.

It sets me thinking of the black American feminist Audre Lorde, who wrote that true love celebrates the sensual but with the heart engaged, while the merely pornographic seeks sensation but without the heart's connection.

Could that be a metaphor for how we choose to live our lives?

Seeking that of God within rather than just using one another?

Jesus loved the little children, and with the summer holidays I'm wondering what it means to care for children better, to cultivate their qualities of heart and build a world of empathy, and reality – not just virtual, but meaningful.

Note:

Audre Lorde can be heard reading her essay 'Uses of the Erotic' at this link: www.youtube.com/watch?v=xFHwg6aNKy0

Seat of the faeries

We're full swing into Scotland's festivals with easily a hundred of them taking place this summer. They're good for entertainment and for the local economy, but I suspect they're also good for something in the soul, the imagination.

When academics try to study Scots creativity they quickly hit upon a sense of magic, so much so that leading scholars hold that the realm of *faerie* is *'a metaphor for the imagination'*.[1]

Last weekend my wife and I went walking in the Blackwood of Rannoch. We booked into a B & B at Dunalastair and our room looked out directly on the concave pointed summit of Schiehallion.

Our host was a retired surveyor. 'So, what does *Schiehallion* mean?' I asked at breakfast time, playing the daft laddie.

'It means,' he said, with a puff of pride: *'the Seat of the Caledonian Faeries.'*

'Oh? And do you believe in the *sìth*[2] – the faeries?'

'Yes!' he proclaimed, followed quickly by: 'Well, OK – you don't believe in the faeries. But you don't disbelieve in them either. *They might be watching!'*

Of course, we were pulling one another's legs – kind of – but truth be told I'd sat up late the night before and watched a waxing moon rise up and hover in the mists above the mountain.

As I turned in I'd thought: *Here is what is meant by the* sìth – *a byword for beauty in nature.*

That night I had a dream. It was about the need for love to be woven in with all our economic activity. So wondrous was the imagery that I was shaken to tears and woke up thinking: 'My goodness – is this what happens when *I to the hills will lift mine eyes*?'

The Scots imagination grows from qualities hidden deep within this land. May such creative roots be shared at all our summer festivals – and remember – *they might be watching.*

Notes:

1. John MacInnes, *Dùthchas Nan Gàidheal: Selected Essays of John MacInnes*, ed. Michael Newton, Birlinn, Edinburgh, 2006, p.467

2. *Sìth*: pronounced shee-h

Power and empowerment

Power is in the news big-time at the moment. Power in the sense of what we're paying for our domestic energy bills. Power as the petrol and diesel refined at Grangemouth, and power of the human kind from both sides of that refinery's industrial dispute.

When yet another energy company announced a ten percent price hike this week I happened to be on the website of Ineos, who own Grangemouth, and I was struck that they list one of their key aspirations as – the *'empowerment of employees'*.

It's an interesting word: *empowerment*. It means to invest with power, to find power with others, and especially, power *from within*.

It happens that my wife and I have found ourselves feeling very empowered this year in the face of ever-rising energy prices. We've managed to make our bills crash through the floor by installing solar panels and a small air-source heat pump. Put simply, the energy of light falling on our roof helps pump heat from the outside and warm the house – even on cold days – and that, with equipment that now costs no more than a decent second-hand car.[1]

I'm not wanting to sound smug; I'm wanting to share experience. Not every home is suitable for renewable energy and many people couldn't afford it, but with the right policies in place these technologies could make a huge difference to cutting greenhouse gas emissions and fuel poverty, because they harness the powers of nature.

In spiritual language, such are the gifts of Providence, and while I don't go along with all of the Westminster Shorter Catechism that we used to learn in school, I do love the part that describes God's presence as manifesting *'in the works of creation and providence'*.

To me, that's the root of real *empowerment*. That's the power that can change the world: God's energy.

Note:

1. See: www.alastairmcintosh.com/general/energy/solar-heating.htm

Who am I to judge?

It's been a weekend of deep, deep contrasts. As the desperate events in Kenya unfolded, there also occurred a quiet moment of potential renewal in the world.

The consecration of Monsignor Leo Cushley as the new Archbishop of the Catholic Church in Scotland fills the post left vacant by Cardinal Keith O'Brien. I imagine that many will have felt great joy, but also, a whirl of emotion about the sexual scandals of recent years.

For some, it will have been the emotion of the unfinished pain and anger of having been abused, but for a great many, the hope that their Church can once again shine out as something beautiful for God.

Sexual abuse is a tragic matter, but diversity in consenting adult sexuality is quite another. On Friday a gay Jewish friend sent me an e-mail saying, 'You got to love that Pope!', because he'd read a remarkable interview where Pope Francis said: '*if a homosexual person is of good will and is in search of God, I am no one to judge … God in creation has set us free: it is not possible to interfere spiritually in the life of a person.*'[1]

But it's not just Roman Catholics who are capable of grappling with challenging issues so graciously. When Cardinal O'Brien resigned I had an e-mail from a conservative evangelical Presbyterian clergyman. He said that, for him, Keith O'Brien's *'hopeless pain overshadows everything'*, and while his critics could be forti-fied in their knowledge that they were right, the Cardinal, having abused trust, could – and I quote: *'resort only to the Apostles' Creed: I believe in the forgiveness of sins'.*

That's what's wonderful about the Christianity – both Catholic and Protestant – that's starting to emerge in today's world. It trumps the weight of judgement; and does so with the saving grace of love.

Note:

1. www.americanmagazine.org/pope-interview

The ark of Syria

For the time being the threat of war with Syria has receded, but this remains a tense week, by the end of which President Assad needs to have provided a full list of his chemical weapons for destruction.

Last week's diplomatic breakthrough was heralded by an unprecedented open letter that President Putin wrote in the *New York Times* to the American people.[1]

In addition to pointing out that the world's religious leaders have urged against war, Putin challenged *'American exceptionalism'.*

This is a notion, based on the thought of some of the founding fathers, that the United States holds a God-given *'manifest destiny'* to act as a *'chosen people'*, shining over and above the other nations.

Putin therefore ended his letter reminding that *'We are all differ-ent, but when we ask for the Lord's blessings, we must not forget that God created us equal.'*

Now, we have every right to be suspicious when a politician

appeals to God, but no right to be cynical. On the contrary, recent days have seen a rare lubrication of international diplomacy; one that reflects well simultaneously on the Russians, the Americans, and, yes, the British Parliament too.

My thoughts move to a seventh-century saint called Isaac of Syria. He saw that peace can only be grown from the tree of love, and he said: '*The ark of Noah was built in the time of peace, and its timbers were planted by him a hundred years beforehand.*'[2]

You or I may not be in a position to produce a quick fix for Syria. But each of us, in our own ways, can plant acorns for the future. As Robert Burns wrote:

Wi' plenty o' sic [such] trees, I trow [trust],
The warld [world] would live in peace, man;
The sword would help to mak [make] a plough,
The din o' war wad [would] cease, man.[3]

Notes:

1. http://www.nytimes.com/2013/09/12/opinion/putin-plea-for-caution-from-russia-on-syria.html?pagewanted=all&_r=2&

2. Taken and slightly adapted from *The Ascetical Homilies of Saint Isaac*, Holy Transfiguration Monastery, 1984.

3. From 'The tree of liberty'

Mothering Sunday

I was searching for a theme for *Thought for the Day*, and was on the phone to my mother, and she said: 'Are you remembering this weekend – is Mothering Sunday?'

Well! She must have known that I was *just about* to go out and buy a card.

But it set my wife, Vérène, and me laughing. And thinking. And then Vérène said that for some women this annual celebration can also have a painful side. For those who may have lost or never known their mother, or not have been able to have children of their own, it can be a time when grief invisible, and hard to talk about, can be reactivated.

I've got two children from my first marriage, but seven years ago Vérène and I lost our only child together in stillbirth.

As we reminisced, a thought came to us: Mothering Sunday differs from the commercialised American invention of Mother's Day. The Sunday is a religious festival with a date that moves each year in step with Easter. It used to be a holiday when labourers returned to their mother's church to reunite the family.

And that begs the question: who is our family? And paradoxically, Jesus didn't teach traditional family values.

The gospels tell how his mother and brothers were worried by all the rumpus being stirred up by his radical teachings. They came to take him home. But he demanded of them: '*Who is my mother, and who are my brethren?*' Then pointing to the crowd he answered: whoever follows God in Heaven '*is my brother, and sister, and mother*'.[1]

In other words, let not our sense of family be too small. God, he taught, is like a mother hen that gathers all beneath her wings, inviting and inciting us to be each other's family.[2]

Well, so much for the theology. But right now, I'd better dash off to buy that card. And as the day approaches, if a certain Jean McIntosh happens to be listening in Stornoway – then, *Happy Mothering Sunday*.

Notes:

1. Matthew 12, Luke 8, Mark 3
2. Matthew 23, Luke 13

The boldness of the Holy Spirit

Just as I was preparing today's 'Thought' an e-mail banged in on my desk from a Presbyterian friend in the Highlands – once a lady of the manse – commenting on this week's remarkable religious news.

The Roman Catholic Church in Scotland has appointed Andrew McLellan, formerly both a Moderator of the Kirk and Chief Inspector of Prisons, to carry out an external review of its procedures for safeguarding vulnerable people against abuse.

'Very ecumenical!' my Highland friend said wryly. 'There will be a lot of bones stirring in the old church – not knowing whether to protest or rejoice.'

To me, as to herself, there's no question that this reflects a joyous softening of the religious divide. It came in the same week as Pope Francis released an astonishing new document called *Evangelii Gaudium – The Joy of the Gospel* – which is being hailed as '*a Magna Carta for church reform*'.[1]

Here the Pope calls for '*a resolute process of discernment, purification and reform*' guided by the boldness (*parrhesia*) of the Holy Spirit.

Francis says: *'I prefer a church which is bruised, hurting and dirty because it has been out on the streets.'* And in a forthright challenge to materialism, he adds: *'The Pope loves everyone, rich and poor alike, but he is obliged in the name of Christ to remind all that the rich must help, respect and promote the poor.'*

Dr McLellan tells me that he was astonished to have been asked to assist his Catholic colleagues. While recognising the pitfalls, he'll build a team and do his best.

May our prayers be with this generous spirit moving within both the Church of Scotland and the Scottish Catholic Church. Purification and reform takes courage, but you don't get courage without a living heart.

Note:

1.http://w2.vatican.va/content/francesco/en/apost_exhortations/documents/pap a-francesco_esortazione-ap_20131124_evangelii-gaudium.html

Wild Goose Publications, the publishing house of the Iona Community established in the Celtic Christian tradition of Saint Columba, produces books, e-books, CDs and digital downloads on:

- holistic spirituality
- social justice
- political and peace issues
- healing
- innovative approaches to worship
- song in worship, including the work of the Wild Goose Resource Group
- material for meditation and reflection

For more information:

Wild Goose Publications
Fourth Floor, Savoy House
140 Sauchiehall Street,
Glasgow G2 3DH, UK

Tel. +44 (0)141 332 6292
Fax +44 (0)141 332 1090
e-mail: admin@ionabooks.com

or visit our website at
www.ionabooks.com
for details of all our products and online sales